COUNTRY LIVING

HOME ALMANAC

Maintaining Your House Month by Month

BY

JOHN GATES

A FAIR STREET BOOK

HEARST BOOKS

A DIVISION OF STERLING PUBLISHING CO., INC.

NEW YORK

Produced by Fair Street Productions
Project Director: Susan Wechsler
Editor: Rachel Carley
Copyeditor: Helen Dunn
Designer: Robert Bull Design
Photo Research: Deborah Anderson/Photosearch, Inc.
Text Coordinator: Shaie Dively

Library of Congress Cataloging-in-Publication Data
Available upon request.

10 9 8 7 6 5 4 3 2 1

Published by Hearst Books,
A Division of Sterling Publishing Company, Inc.
387 Park Avenue South, New York, N.Y. 10016

Country Living and Hearst Books are trademarks owned by
Hearst Magazines Property, Inc., in USA, and Hearst Communications, Inc., in Canada.

Distributed in Canada by Sterling Publishing
c/o Canadian Manda Group, One Atlantic Avenue, Suite 105
Toronto, Ontario, Canada M6K 3E7
Distributed in Australia by Capricorn Link (Australia) Pty. Ltd.
P.O. Box 704, Windsor, NSW 2756 Australia

Manufactured in China

ISBN 1-58816-212-5

Contents

Foreword

The old saying that it pays to meet the right people is never truer than when it comes to contractors—which is why we are so delighted to introduce you to one of the best we know. John Gates is not only a walking encyclopedia of everything there is to learn about home building and maintenance, but also an indispensable resource of information gained through decades of experience on the job. Descended from a long line of builders and woodworkers, he is a talented craftsman in his own right, and his deep respect for home and family contributes to an innate appreciation for the seasonal routines and traditions that are part and parcel of home ownership. Like most people we know, he also derives enormous satisfaction from a well-kept house.

It is our particular pleasure, then, to share the expertise of this valued member of the *Country Living* family in our new month-by-month guide to home care.

To help you prioritize and organize the many jobs that go into keeping home and yard in shape over the course of a year, we begin each month with a checklist of tasks. Read on and you will find a wealth of practical information concerning the inner workings of your house, including those mysterious plumbing, heating, and electrical systems. Landscape care and gardening are also covered in depth in this indispensable calendar of advice.

At the risk of boasting, we think that our *Home Almanac* is the most comprehensive, user-friendly home guide around. And best of all, this is one calendar that will never go out of date! We hope you will learn from reading and using it as much as we have in putting it together.

—Nancy Mernit Soriano,
Editor-in-Chief, *Country Living*

Introduction

As I look around my shop, I spot my great-grandfather's adze hanging just below his broadaxe. I can't resist picking up this tool and holding it just as he did, hundreds of times, during his career as a barn builder in upstate New York. I marvel at the smooth shape of the hand-forged head, secured to the worn wood handle by a wedge of leather. How often

by the one-room schoolhouse to tell the teacher that his son, Leonard James Gates— my grandfather—would not be returning to his studies until the middle of April. Having reached the third grade, Leonard James was old enough to learn his trade as a barn builder, and he was needed to cut and finish the heavy framing timbers for the next season's barn raisings.

both parts must have been replaced, worn out from the thousands of swings against the tough oak timbers in the frigid Adirondack winters. Holding that adze reminds me what a privilege it is to be a fourth-generation carpenter in a line of woodworkers extending back to England over hundreds of years.

My great-grandfather, Cranston Gates, and his father owned a sawmill at Gates Corners in Jefferson County, New York. There, the family milled finishing lumber and floorboards for the houses and barns that sheltered farmers and their animals from the harsh St. Lawrence River valley weather. When leaves blew dry across the ground and deepening frost hardened the earth, Cranston Gates set up winter camp in the north woods. On the way, he stopped

The camp was near a good stand of oaks and a running stream that supplied an unfrozen water source throughout the winter. Trees were cut, hewn into squared timbers, sized and shaped, and laid out in the geometric "bents" that formed the structural backbone of barns and houses. All winter long father and son labored with crosscut saws, felling axes and broadaxes, smoothing adzes, mortising chisels, wooden mallets, and other hand tools to fill orders for barns and outbuildings that would be erected in late spring and summer.

After the completed bents were fitted together, a marking adze was used to score the parts at each mortise-and-tenon joint with matching numbers so that the timbers could be reassembled for a perfect fit many miles away.

Because the ground was still frozen, horses could skid the disassembled bents to the edge of the forest before the first traces of spring thaw marked the end of winter camp.

While the frames were loaded into wagons and delivered to customers eagerly awaiting their new barns, my grandfather went back to school to finish up the year. Come summer, he returned to work with his father to erect the structures planned in their minds and assembled on the forest floor a few months earlier. Grandpa's job was to drive in the wooden pegs, known as "tenons" or "trunnels," to draw up and secure the mortised joints. Because there were no nails to rust and the joints were so tight, many barns built in this manner are still standing strong and solid. Only through neglect do they slowly sink into the earth.

This stage in my family's history is the genesis of my father's favorite saying: "The Gateses build forever." Our family has always understood that the quality and honest hard work built into a structure create a sense of permanence—something to be proud of many years later. We work hard and stay with a job until it's done. Characteristic of the North Country, these qualities are also strong in the Gates family.

My grandfather's hard work and training paid off. In time, Leonard James became a well-known contractor in the St. Lawrence valley. At the turn of the 19th century, he was hired to build a pulpwood loading trestle and docking station in the village of Cape Vincent. His bright red wagon and handsome black horse created quite a stir when he arrived in town. He commanded everyone's attention, but it was Edna Vearrette who caught *his* eye. Recently arrived from Canada, my grandmother was working at a seed-packing plant not far from the pulpwood project. Grandpa lived in Carthage, just east of Watertown, and when he headed home after a long week's work and a short visit with his future bride, he often fell asleep sitting on the wagon bench. Fortunately, the horse knew the way home—all 30 miles.

My father, Leonard Cranson Gates, was Leonard James's and Edna's third child. Born sickly, he could not digest milk, and the doctor was sure he would not live very long. His Aunt Nonny nourished him with barley water, and he is now 88 years old—a retired carpenter, builder, and civil engineer.

All four of Grandpa's children graduated from college at a time when it was rare, especially for women, to earn a degree. His own education was repeatedly interrupted before it ended at about the fifth grade, and he insisted that all his children have the opportunity to complete college. My father's older sister, Kathryn, graduated first and helped to put her two younger brothers and sister through school. Kathryn, known as Aunt Kotty, is now 93 and lives in Watertown; she is still very special to my father and to me.

The stories of my parents, aunts and uncles, grandparents, great-grandparents, and all the Gateses before me have instilled in me the appreciation for tradition and family that inspired me to write this almanac. Seasonal routines like cleaning in the spring and raking leaves in the fall link us to culture and landscape in a reassuringly tangible way. It's not hard to understand why a commuter sitting in highway traffic for two hours on a summer afternoon yearns to be in the seat of his (or her) lawn tractor instead. Caring for home and garden offers a welcome break from the regular workday and also gives us a chance to slow the pace and take control of our lives.

All these years of experience have taught me that people who own their homes instinctively accept the responsibility that ownership requires. Indeed, building or buying a house is the single most important investment most people will ever make. Caring for it is a way of protecting that investment—and also a matter of pride. As a contractor and builder, I have a professional reputation to uphold. And like my father, grandfather, and great-grandfather, I want to see a job done well.

Most of the suggestions that you will find on the following pages come directly from my own experience as both a builder and a homeowner. The month-by-month breakdown of tasks is designed to make it easy for you to prioritize. Each chapter begins with a checklist to give you a quick overview of tasks for that month. The monthly maintenance tips are expanded and organized in a logical progression moving from indoors to outdoors—complete with suggestions for your yard and garden. Following these sections, look for related, in-depth features devoted to history, design advice, and practical explanations of the inner workings of your house.

These features also cover safety concerns. When caring for your home, you can tackle many jobs yourself, but be aware of your limitations and always make safety your primary concern. If you botch the living room paint job, no real harm has been done; but plumbing, electricity, roofing, and heating are complicated tasks. Never attempt any job that requires skill, knowledge, or tools you don't have! Ask for help or hire a professional. When you seek expert help, be sure to get references and check them carefully. The cream will rise to the top in your search for a good person for the job. Most important, remember that we should all take pleasure in caring for our homes. Consistency, common sense, knowledge, and perseverance are the keys to a safe and happy household.

—John Gates

Acknowledgments

To Aunt Kotty — who fostered my life-long interest in reading and nourished my love of heritage with her boundless treasury of family lore.

I could not have completed this project without the gracious help of so many people.

I offer thanks to: Rachel Carley, whose unending patience and great writing talent put my ideas in readable form on the pages of this book; Betty Rice of Hearst Books for her belief in the idea and her continued support; *Country Living* magazine for sponsoring the book; Bob Bull who made everything look so much better with his layout and design skill.

I am especially indebted to Susan Wechsler of Fair Street Productions, for giving me this opportunity, and for her encouraging guidance throughout the entire process.

Most of what appears in this book is taken from my own experience. I am indebted to all the craftsmen who over the years shared their knowledge and skills, contributing to my education as a builder. My parents nurtured my curiosity and taught me the value of hard work and honest dealings. I am perpetually grateful to them for these gifts and for their constant love and support.

My deepest gratitude goes to my wife and life partner, Sharon, for her love is the steady presence that enriches my life and makes all things worthwhile.

HOME*A*LMANAC

Maintaining Your House Month by Month

WINTER

Blanketing winter snows make us think of crackling fires, good books, and restful days after a busy fall of projects in and around the house. Some people who live in northern latitudes find winter a period of quiet hibernation—a time to enjoy sleepy solitude and dormant days while waiting out the cold. Others consider the winter months a useful part of the calendar year for home maintenance. My grandfather was one of those people. For a barn builder, cold weather was actually the best time for cutting trees and preparing timbers, which is why this job was traditionally done in the dead of winter. In fact, Grampa saw winter as the "easy time." The wood was lighter than in spring when the sap was running, and the ice-slicked snow made the logs skid faster.

Given that I descend from such a long line of hard workers, winding down completely is probably not a realistic option for me: The penchant for productivity is too deeply embedded in my genes. I may not be harvesting oaks deep in the wilderness of upstate New York, but I do schedule heavy tree pruning in my own yard, trimming weak or dead limbs and stacking them to dry and "season" for next year's firewood. The cold winter air also gives my family the feeling that it's fine for all of us to take advantage of indoor time.

Consider this to be the season for indoor projects like organizing closets, refinishing the blanket chest that has been gathering dust in the attic, or tackling any of the dozens of tasks that you set aside when the summer weather beckoned you outdoors. The secret is to divide your time between that crackling fire and the projects that make winter your "easy time" inside or out. At this time of year, it's good to enjoy both sides of the window.

THINGS TO DO IN JANUARY

INSIDE

- Organize paperwork.
- Deodorize rugs and carpets.
- Run your humidifier.
- Disinfect against colds and flu.
- Purify the air with houseplants.
- Dress up closet shelves.

OUTSIDE

- Look for ice dams and water leaks.
- Check your security system.
- Inspect the roof and gutters.

DECK, PORCH, AND PATIO

- Guard against uneven snow accumulation.
- Avoid stacking wood where it will create snow buildup.
- Plan storage.

GARAGE AND TOOLSHED

- Have snow- and ice-clearing equipment in good order.
- Invest in a good stepladder.
- Straighten up your work area.

YARD AND LANDSCAPE

- Make sure snow is cleared away from your mailbox.
- Brush excess snow off shrubs and foundation plants.
- Use discarded holiday greens for winter plant bedding.
- Keep an eye out for dead and broken tree branches.
- Be aware of freeze-thaw cycles.

January

*T*he end of the holiday season once seemed a bit of a letdown—but that was before I owned my home. These days, not only does January represent a new start in the calendar year for our family, but it's also a great time to sit by the fire and dream up some new projects. Your New Year's resolutions, of course, can always include tackling those tasks that never quite got done last year.

■ **Organize paperwork.** Throughout the year you should be keeping track of expenses for improvements and repairs that may be tax deductible. Because the cost of certain home improvements can be included when you calculate capital gains and losses on a future sale, keeping good records is important. January is the logical time to separate and file bills and expenses incurred during the preceding year. Start a file box or drawer specifically for this purpose and, while you're at it, organize and file your operating manuals and warranties for household appliances. Most manuals offer valuable maintenance advice. Take an afternoon to read through them and note any seasonal tips. Check the expiration dates of warranties, which are usually linked to date of purchase. Some warranties offer extensions, and it may be time to apply.

■ **Deodorize rugs and carpets.** This should be done periodically throughout the year, and the post–Christmas party season is a good time to begin. Starting the year with fresh carpets is a great feeling because your whole house will smell better. Use a commercial product or deodorize naturally by sprinkling on a light layer of baking soda. Leave the soda on for a couple of hours to allow it to absorb odors, then vacuum it up.

■ **Run your humidifier.** You can minimize the seasonal expand-contract cycle that occurs in a heated house by using a humidifier to moisten the air—which is as good for your own health as it is for your home's. The dry heat produced by furnaces, boilers, and electrical heating systems can be a real problem. A particular casualty

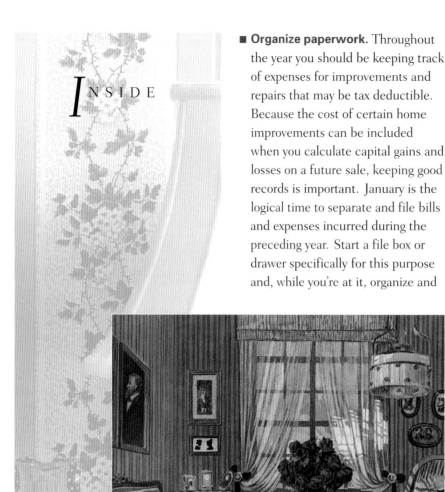

(other than your family's sinuses) is wood, which will shrink in dry conditions. Dry air can actually cause paneling to loosen, paint to crack, and tabletops and chair legs to split. Changes in humidity can also make a piano go out of tune.

The moisture that a humidifier adds to the air helps prevent these problems while alleviating static electricity. Some heating and air-conditioning systems have built-in humidifiers, but these are expensive and complex to install if they're not already part of the system. Consider buying a small console (floor model) or a portable type. Theoretically, one humidifier should do the job (start with one in the master bedroom), but if your house is too dry, you may want to add a second humidifier. Try installing one on each floor. Mark the beginning of the year by running a maintenance check. Be sure to follow manufacturer's instructions for cleaning to prevent buildup of bacteria.

■ **Disinfect against colds and flu.** To help prevent the spread of winter afflictions, pay particular attention to areas where germs and bacteria may be lurking. In the kitchen target countertops, the refrigerator door, and cabinet and oven handles.

Wash these areas with a store-bought disinfectant or use a diluted bleach solution (¾ cup bleach to 1 gallon water). You can use the same bleach solution to sanitize kitchen and bathroom drains. In your bathrooms tackle the toilet, sink, tub, shower, and faucets. Disinfect doorknobs throughout the house.

TIP The Natural Way If you're bothered by the fumes in commercial cleansers, try scrubbing sinks and tubs with a natural abrasive: Table salt and baking soda are nontoxic alternatives. Baking soda (sodium bicarbonate) is also good for deodorizing drains and refrigerators and for removing stains from tile and porcelain.

■ **Purify the air with houseplants.** Research by scientists at NASA shows that potted plants absorb many invisible but common household gases, including the formaldehyde that is commonly "outgassed" from building materials, carpets, and manufactured cabinetry and furniture. English ivy, areca and bamboo palms, and rubber plants are among the plants known to filter toxins efficiently.

■ **Dress up closet shelves.** Why not? If you're stuck indoors on a rotten day, you can cheer yourself up by tackling a manageable task that yields quick, gratifying results. Line closet shelves with fresh, lightly scented shelf paper and add an inexpensive paper trim. Organize the contents by category—towels, washcloths, fitted sheets, flat sheets, blankets, quilts—then mark the shelves with neatly written labels. Smaller items can go in baskets or bandboxes.

BASKETS

Many people associate baskets with summer decorating, but these collectibles can also look great in the winter—especially when filled with a simple arrangement of dried greens or flowers (eucalyptus or hydrangea, say) or a pile of winter squash or polished apples. When using or displaying baskets during cold weather, however, be aware that the drying effects of radiators, woodstoves, and fireplace heat can do serious damage to the fibers. Always keep baskets away from any heating element and out of direct sunlight, which can fade the colors of stains and paint finishes. Some experts recommend rejuvenating a dried-out basket by misting it lightly or placing it in a steam-filled bathroom for a few minutes; but this treatment is only for baskets that are not painted or colored in any way.

Dust baskets gently with a new paintbrush or a feather duster and remove stains with a damp cloth, testing first in an inconspicuous spot. If gentle rubbing seems to do the job without damaging the finish or leaving a water mark, clean the stain and dry the basket immediately. (If you have any doubts, leave it alone.) Never try to protect a basket by applying a coat of varnish, shellac, or lacquer, though, because these can damage fibers by preventing them from absorbing moisture from the air.

If you want to expand or start a basket collection, remember that a winter weekend is a great time to do some hunting at an antiques fair or auction; you may even find a few bargains after the Christmas season is over. Look for examples with an unusual shape or an original finish (original paint will typically show signs of wear on the handles, rim, and bottom); both contribute to the value of a piece. Even though it is unusual to find a basket that dates from before the mid- to late-1800s, the range of styles and types available is vast—this is mainly because thousands of baskets were made as part of a widespread American cottage industry that thrived into the early 1900s.

Among the most common were woven splint baskets, used for gathering fruits and vegetables and for storing and carrying household items and farm produce. Such utilitarian pieces were sold door-to-door, in shops, and through mail order. The beautifully crafted forms produced for sale by the Shakers and the painted and potato-stamped baskets made by Native Americans are in great demand by collectors.

CARING FOR WOOD PANELING

Wood paneling is an important decorative feature of your home that can and should be protected—usually by sealing the wood with varnish or finishing it with wax or oil. Not only are such treatments good for paneling, but they can also produce a mellow luster. The choices vary and are somewhat subjective—a glossy urethane finish, for example, has a more contemporary feel than the more traditional glow of wax or oil. If you're not starting from scratch, a good, safe rule of thumb is to go with whatever is there. Most finishes darken the wood, but time and sunlight will darken it more than anything you apply with a rag or brush.

In general, wood paneling needs little more than cleaning to maintain the existing finish. Any finish protected with wax should be dusted and polished only. Otherwise, I recommend Murphy Oil Soap, which is a pure vegetable oil, and a soft cloth for cleaning wood that has been treated with varnishes, shellacs, and oils.

When the finish has lost its luster, you may need to apply a new finishing coat. This requires preparing the surface, usually by going over it lightly and evenly with fine sandpaper or steel wool. If necessary, touch up scratches with a stain in a matching color. Then gently wipe away the sanding residue with a tack cloth and reapply a fresh varnish or other finish, following the manufacturer's directions. If you are using a wax or oil polish for added protection, choose a good furniture-grade product like Minwax.

Here's my favorite recipe for a homemade wood sealer and finish coat that yields a traditional Williamsburg look: a simple solution of one part turpentine and one part boiled linseed oil. Make sure to use boiled, not raw, linseed oil (check the label); the raw oil won't soak in as well, and it will take forever to dry. Rub the solution into the wood using a soft clean cloth, let it soak in, then rub again just before it gets sticky. If it's too sticky, try wetting the cloth with a little more oil or a dab of turpentine. My technique is to try to rub *all* the oil off, as though I didn't want any there.

This technique produces a really good polish, because the pressure and the heat generated when you rub helps the oil to penetrate while bringing out the grain of the wood. It will take several coats—at least three—and an hour or two for each to achieve a real depth to the finish, but it is well worth the effort. In general, the more coats, the shinier the surface. The old rule for linseed oil was to apply it once a week for a month, once a month for a year, and then once a year. Polishing with wax is admittedly quicker and easier, but the surface always needs more waxing, and the wax has a tendency to collect dust. With linseed oil you apply less, rather than more, over time, and the old-fashioned finish looks better and better with each passing day.

OUTSIDE

■ **Look for ice dams and water leaks.** An ice dam occurs when warm air escapes into the attic, melting snow on the roof. At the same time, the roof eaves are surrounded by cold air; when the water runs down to the eaves, it may freeze on the overhang before it can drain into your gutters or drip to the ground. As the resulting ice dam builds up, it continues to trap the running water behind it, forcing it back and up under the bottom edge of the shingles. Eventually, the water will leak over the top edge of the roof shingles and work its way into the house. To remove an ice dam, you'll need to climb a ladder and crack it gently to relieve the pressure behind the dam. Do this *very* carefully with a hammer or other blunt tool to avoid damage to the roofing materials. (If you leave the ice to melt on its own, the leak may worsen.) You might also consider spraying hot water on the ice to melt it.

■ **Check your security system.** Snow, wind, rain, and ice can damage exterior sensors. Test the system. If you have motion detectors or sensors in the driveway or on walkways, test them to see if they are operating correctly. Make sure the exterior siren sounds and has not been damaged by the elements.

■ **Inspect the roof and gutters.** This check is especially important after heavy storms. Keep gutters clear of debris and see that all water is draining properly off the roof and away from the sides of your house.

FANLIGHTS

One of the most distinctive and recognizable exterior features of Colonial houses is the semicircular window often found above the front entry and known logically as a fanlight (literally, a fan-shaped "light," or window). Before the era of electricity, a window over the door served the practical purpose of letting daylight into an otherwise dark entry passage and might be supplemented by sidelights (flanking the door). The use of a fan-shaped light (as opposed to a simple rectangle) reflected the decorative influence of the English Georgian style (prevalent from about 1720 to 1780) and the later Federal style (circa 1780 to 1820). The Federal-era fan designs are often flatter and more elongated; the earlier Georgian-style fans are rounded. Throughout both periods, a fanlight was also often incorporated into the gable end of the house to light the attic and provide a strong decorative element on the upper story.

Though the fanlight dividers, or muntins, are often wood, original windows from the 18th and 19th centuries can display particularly lovely designs in lead. Lead muntins are prone to damage from snow and ice, so if you are lucky enough to own a house with an old leaded fanlight, try to brush snow off before it freezes and causes the lead to break or buckle. But if the window ices over, leave it alone.

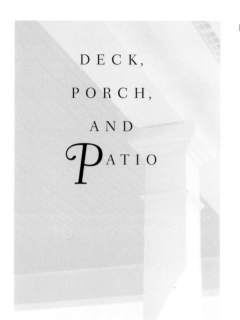

DECK, PORCH, AND $\mathcal{P}$ATIO

■ **Guard against uneven snow accumulation.** It's easy to let snow pile up on decks, patios, and porches, particularly since you may not be using these outdoor areas during the winter. Shovel periodically to prevent the snow and ice from damaging wood surfaces. Light snow on stone or brick pavers acts like a blanket to reduce frost action, but the key is to keep the snow level even. If part of the patio is clear and part covered with piles of snow, the uncovered pavers are likely to lift more than the buried ones. Don't leave piles of snow near any door: They create a safety

hazard. Melting snow can also leak around the sill, causing water damage inside your home.

■ **Avoid stacking wood where it will create snow buildup.** You may need to replenish your supply of cordwood after the holidays, but resist the temptation to pile wood wherever is easiest—for example, on your back porch. After one storm, a stack of wood stored near a door or on a weakened deck can become one big ice and snow problem. Wood is heavy, and an overload can crack or otherwise damage patio pavers or the wood flooring of a deck or porch. Pile the wood nearby in your yard, and bring small loads to the door as you need them.

■ **Plan storage.** Think back to last summer: What was your deck or patio missing? If you have the space, consider adding cupboards or a couple of lidded benches that can double as storage for cushions or barbecue gadgets. If built-ins don't suit your budget, scout in your attic or basement for an old piece of furniture—maybe a small chest or bureau that can be used under the shelter of a porch roof. Spend a winter weekend painting or stenciling it and you'll have a great storage piece.

HOW TO HIRE A CONTRACTOR

What's the best way to find and work effectively with a contractor? Surprisingly, this remains one of the great mysteries of home improvement projects. It's remarkable that so many people are willing to trust one of their largest lifetime investments—building a house or an addition—to a stranger without knowing how to protect that investment or how to get the results they want. A common pitfall is to think that trusting the job entirely to someone relieves us of the pressure of worrying. It's easy to say to yourself, "He or she is good, so I can leave it all up to him or her." This is a huge mistake, even if your contractor is good and trustworthy. You *must* be involved and understand the process or have someone on your side who does.

The first and most important step in working well with a contractor is choosing the right one: That means (1) the right contractor for the type and size of the job; (2) one with a reputation for quality work, fairness, and the ability to get along with suppliers and clients; and (3) someone with whom *you* can get along.

Using the first two criteria, begin your search by developing a list of recommendations from neighbors, friends, and acquaintances—your lawyer, your accountant, your grocer, your barber. Based on your research, you'll ultimately want to solicit three to five estimates, or bids, for the job (see "The Bidding Process," October). You can also solicit names at your local lumberyard or even ask at job sites.

Once you have narrowed the choice to a few candidates, arrange a meeting and try to get a sense of how compatible you are. Inquire about the location of current and recently completed jobs and ask the contractor to make an appointment with these clients (or get permission to call yourself) so that you can see the work firsthand. Make the visit to the site without the contractor present; the owners will be more open in their opinions.

Ask questions. Is the work of good quality? (If you can't tell, take someone with you who can.) Does the job site look neat and safe? Are materials stored properly, or scattered and disorganized? Are the workers clean and neat? Do they look interested in their jobs? Does the contractor answer phone calls promptly? Is there someone responsible (in charge) on the job every day? How does the contractor deal with problems? Does he or she suggest alternatives or constructive changes to improve efficiency or save some money? Is the project on budget, or are the extras adding up? Have problems come up and if so, were they fixed? Did the contractor respond with quick, friendly concern or with disinterest and excuses?

Be aware that no matter how good and conscientious a contractor is, nothing ever goes perfectly—especially with so many people, jobs, and materials involved. Difficulties are always going to come up. The better the contractor, however, the fewer the problems, and the less severe. The important thing is that he or she arrive promptly on the job to solve the problem.

Speaking of "she," this is a good place to point out that women used to be rare in this business, and even rarer as GCs (general contractors) or as heads of subcontracting businesses; but more are arriving on the scene each day. Most women I've encountered make very good contractors. This observation may be disconcerting to the old-boy crowd, but I find women in the business to be very trustworthy, organized, and skillful in dealing with their clients.

That is where the third criterion comes in. The main concern is to make sure that you and your contractor have an excellent rapport. Discuss details and "what-ifs" to see if you can deal comfortably throughout the project. If you can't discuss the work openly and honestly with each other now, things could get worse when a problem arises. And don't forget: The contractor is also checking you out to see whether you will be a difficult customer.

TIP Getting Recommendations Although contractors do advertise in the newspaper and Yellow Pages, in my experience the good ones don't advertise much, if at all, unless they also sell a product as part of their service (such as a line of windows, kitchen cabinets, or greenhouses). A personal recommendation is always more reliable. But remember: Few people will admit that they picked the wrong contractor or that they think the work is substandard because they're embarrassed or feel the choice reflects poorly on their own decision-making. You may have to use your intuition to interpret their real feelings. Take heed if someone making a recommendation seems hesitant or reluctant to talk openly.

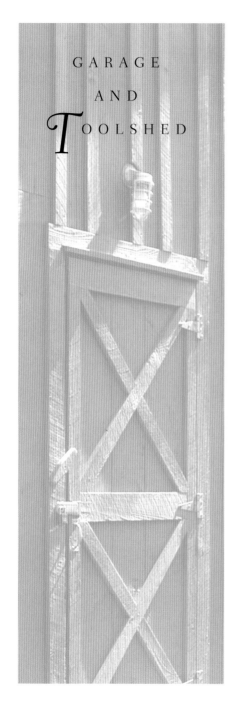

GARAGE AND *T*OOLSHED

- **Have snow- and ice-clearing equipment in good order.** This is the season for early winter storms, when snow shovels and ice choppers should be out of storage and easily accessible. Make sure your tools are in good working condition. If handles are loose, check with a hardware store about replacements before investing in an entirely new tool.

- **Invest in a good stepladder.** This is arguably the most important piece of equipment you can own besides what fits in your toolbox. If you own only one, a six-foot ladder is a good choice, because it's not too unwieldy to fold and carry around. Look for a ladder that does not sway or "walk" across the floor as you move around on it. It should have a fairly wide stance to keep it from tipping and should pivot easily to allow you to open it without trouble. A fold-down tray where you can rest paint cans and tools is also important.

TIP Generators A generator is good for your house and for your peace of mind. Some models are designed to come on automatically, providing an instant backup when you lose electrical power—important in the winter, when a prolonged outage means losing heat, and in summer, when everything in your refrigerator will spoil. Generators come in many forms, with varying capacities (usually measured in hundreds to thousands of watts). A stationary generator can serve your whole house, and a small portable model is handy for providing temporary power in an area where you don't normally have electrical outlets—in the backyard, for example. Consult a reputable supplier about your potential needs. Though a professional should install your generator, you should be familiar with its operation and maintenance needs. Start and test it at least four times a year—more in severe climates—and keep extra parts, like belts and spark plugs, on hand.

■ **Straighten up your work area.** A winter day is a great time to tidy the tool bench and spruce up some of those tools you seldom use but want to have ready when you need them. Sharpen your chisels, clean the dried paint off the putty knife, and fix the frayed power cord on your favorite drill. Charge batteries for the cordless screwdriver and sort all those jars of nails and screws so you can find the size you need.

YARD AND *L*ANDSCAPE

■ **Make sure snow is cleared away from your mailbox.** Mail carriers should have clear access to your box; otherwise they might simply return your mail to the post office. Shovel a wide area around the box support, especially after the snow plow trucks come by, and make sure the door doesn't get frozen shut.

■ **Brush excess snow off shrubs and foundation plants.** The winter-dry branches of dormant shrubs can break under the weight of snow, particularly as it hardens a day or two after falling. Foundation plantings are vulnerable to damage from snow clumps and icicles crashing down from the roof. Plants have a better

chance of coming through unscathed if they are not already encased in a brittle snow coat, so it's a good idea to brush the snow off. Ice, on the other hand, is best left to melt on its own, because the chipping or scraping necessary to get it off can do the plant more harm than good.

- **Use discarded holiday greens for winter plant bedding**. It's an old New England tradition: Before throwing out your Christmas tree, trim off boughs to use as a covering for your garden beds. The greens provide a warm, protective covering for plants and help keep them from heaving out of the soil during a thaw. If you don't plan on recycling greens, see if your town has a program to collect Christmas trees to be chipped for mulch and other uses.

- **Keep an eye out for dead and broken tree branches**. Walk your property and survey for snow and ice damage, especially around power and phone lines. You'll want to prune any split or hanging limbs to prevent further damage to the tree (or anything underneath) if and when they fall.

- **Be aware of freeze-thaw cycles.** These changes in temperature can cause the shrubs that you planted last fall to heave out of the ground. During a thaw, gently work any heaved plants back into the soil and prune broken twigs and branches. It's also a good idea to water broad-leaved and needled evergreens during a thaw to prevent scorching. Trees transpire moisture during a warm spell and are unable to replace it from the frozen ground.

TIP Safety Check After a blizzard, heavy snow, or a bad freezing spell, make sure your water pipes are all in working order. Report downed power lines and broken gas lines immediately. If there are no other problems, wait for streets to open officially before you try to drive anywhere.

THINGS TO DO IN FEBRUARY

INSIDE

- Service your woodstove.
- Think curtains.
- Become an indoor gardener.
- Collect garden catalogues.
- Monitor relative humidity levels.
- Check pumps.

OUTSIDE

- Check bulbs in outdoor fixtures.
- Remove debris outside the clothes dryer vent.

DECK, PORCH, AND PATIO

- Use your gas grill.
- Store propane tanks safely.
- Identify areas that need more lighting in the dark of winter.

GARAGE AND TOOLSHED

- Give your tools a once-over.
- Organize your potting bench.

YARD AND LANDSCAPE

- Check driveway and other markers.
- Continue your yard and garden survey.
- Check the edges of steps, walkways, and your driveway.
- Stay off frozen grass.
- Prune fruit trees.
- Clean your birdhouses.

February

My grandfather used to say that the only good thing about February is that it has fewer days than any other month. The month can certainly be drab—in my part of the world, anyway—but I find that the gray days go by faster when I take on small projects indoors. Completing a task that I have started, like reorganizing a closet or cleaning my workshop, can be quite satisfying. And during one of those brief February thaws you can always get out into the garden on some pretense of early cleanup; even if more snow is in the offing, you'll feel as though you've gotten a head start on spring.

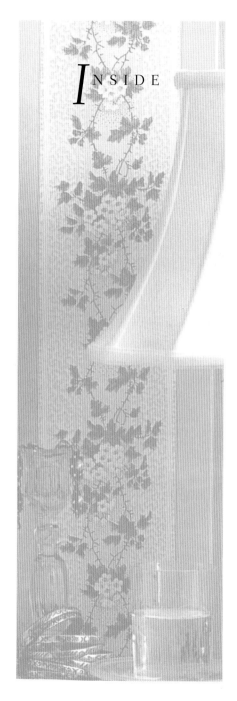

I NSIDE

■ **Service your woodstove.** If you use a woodstove regularly, you should empty it of ash, and clean the doors and the chimney at least twice during the heating season—and once again in the fall before the first use. In particular, check for creosote on the inside of the flue and damper. This gummy black or brown residue, which is produced when wood burns, builds up faster in a woodstove than in a regular fireplace because a wood stove burns more efficiently than a fireplace and sends more heat into a room. The exhausted smoke is cooler and has less air volume, so the chimney is cooler, causing more condensation of gases and creosote.

To remove creosote from a woodstove chimney, you can use a long-handled brush designed for the job. You need a ladder because you'll be cleaning from the roof down. If you try to clean from the bottom of the chimney flue via the stove, you will likely get a face full of soot. Going in from the chimney top allows you to keep the stove doors shut. If you have any doubts about how to do this, hire a professional. (See "Chimney Sweeps," September).

■ **Think curtains.** People used to change curtains by season, switching from summer-weight to heavyweight draperies when cold weather arrived. Most of us have fallen out of that habit, but you should be aware that curtains and blinds are very good heat regulators if they're properly installed and used.

During cold weather, keep curtains and blinds open to let in the sun's warmth, but close them as soon as daylight fades to preserve that warmth. A key addition to any window treatment is a valance. Besides lending a finished look, it also provides "dead air" space, which is an important insulating component. Without a valance, curtains and blinds can actually create a reverse "chimney effect" when they are drawn. Traveling in from the top, warm air funnels downward between the curtain or blind and the window. As heat is lost through the window glass, the air is cooled, then flows down, funneling out from the base of the curtains into the room. This convection process can have a significant effect if there are a lot of windows (especially tall ones) in a room.

Although you want to block airflow, window treatments shouldn't be too "tight." If there is no breathing room, condensation will form on the window glass, staining the sill. Open curtains and blinds just a bit to prevent condensation.

TIP Keeping Air Moist If you use a woodstove, you've probably noticed that it has a real drying effect on the air inside your home. The simple tried-and-true remedy is to put a pot of water on top of the stove. Decorative cast-iron woodstove "steamers" are also available. And get a humidifier!

■ **Become an indoor gardener.** Not only are plants useful as air purifiers, but indoor gardening can be a great antidote to the winter blahs. Treat yourself to some new potted houseplants. Check the soil and leaves (tops and bottoms) of all your indoor plants for aphids, mealybugs, scale, and whiteflies. If a plant is infected, move it away from the healthy ones and treat it with an insecticide solution made specially for houseplants. Check often for watering needs; plants can dry out quickly when the furnace is going.

TIP Keeping Plants Clean

Dust and grime are harmful to houseplants because they compromise the plant's ability to absorb water and sunlight. You can clean most potted plants safely by spritzing them with water or gently wiping the leaves with a damp cloth. Some plants, such as African violets, should be brushed dry to prevent the leaves from developing brown patches.

■ **Collect garden catalogues**. Your mailbox is full of catalogues this time of year, and they can be full of ideas. Seed and plant catalogues arrive early in the winter, and it's not too soon to start making choices. Order as early as possible, before things get sold out. Some catalogues are as useful as magazines for inspiring ideas: You can see garden bed layouts, learn how containers are planted, and even get ideas for porch and deck designs. Tear out pages and file them by category.

■ **Monitoring relative humidity levels.** You can do this simply by picking up a "humidiguide" or hygrometer (essentially a humidity gauge that works like a thermometer) at your local hardware store. Keeping air moist inside your home can help you cut heating costs by maintaining a uniform heating level. The general rule of thumb is to keep a moisture level of 30 percent to 50 percent. Readings will vary, depending on how tight your house is and what kind of heating system you have (woodstoves tend to dry out air the most). Note the obvious indicators; if moisture starts to condense around the base of the humidifier or on picture glass, windows, or ceilings and walls, the level is definitely set too high (see "Run your humidifier," January).

■ **Check pumps for indoor systems that you may need later in the winter or in early spring.** If you have a sump pump, switch it on and run it briefly to make sure it is operating correctly. If you have a dehumidifier pump, also known as a condensation pump, check to see that it is hooked up and ready to run. These pumps drain water from a central dehumidifying system out through your plumbing system, or to the outside.

DUTCH TILES

Among the most distinguished early ceramic wares that Europeans imported to this country were earthenware tiles of Dutch origin or influence. Used to protect floors, walls, and baseboards against moisture, tiles were an integral part of Dutch domestic design in a country where so many settlements originated on floodplains. The ceramic wares provided valuable protection against seeping water, and also became an important decorative element; their manufacture was elevated to a high level of craftsmanship.

Some of the principal tile-making regions in the Netherlands in the 17th century were Delft, Haarlem, Rotterdam, and Utrecht. Although there were many other production centers, Delft is most readily associated with the manufacture of tin-glazed earthenware because of the high-quality tiles made there for export. Earthenware readily absorbs heat, so tiles were also used to build and decorate woodstoves in the Netherlands and throughout the forested northern European countries. The tiles soaked up

heat from a hot, fast-burning wood fire, then radiated warmth into the room for many hours after the fire had burned out. The same principle applies to soapstone woodstoves, which were also used throughout Europe and are now becoming popular in this country.

In Colonial America, Delft tiles typically appeared as fireplace facings. The origin of the blue-and-white patterns associated with the ceramics coincided with the United Dutch East India Company's importation of decorated Chinese porcelain to Europe by the beginning of the 1620s. The tin-glazed earthenware developed by the Dutch offered a much less expensive alternative to the Chinese wares. During the political upheavals of the 17th century, the tile makers and their craft heritage spread through the northern Netherlands into England, Germany, and many other countries. Although authentic antique Dutch tiles are relatively scarce, the national craft tradition has continued, and contemporary tiles with centuries-old designs are readily available.

HIRING A PROFESSIONAL HOUSE CLEANER

For some people, the February thaw brings on the urge for early spring cleaning. If you're thinking of hiring a professional service—for a onetime job or for regular cleanings throughout the year—you should consider the following points before signing anyone on. Start by asking questions:

■ Request references. Be sure to ask for the phone numbers of at least two customers—and don't be timid about calling them. Inquire about the honesty, reliability, and integrity of these potential employees, as well as the care and respect they show for private property. Remember: They are going to have a (more or less) free run of your house.

■ Ask for a written estimate and be sure you know what is covered in the fee. Are you to be charged hourly or by the job? What form of payment is accepted (cash or check), and when is it expected?

■ Chances are that your house cleaners really *don't* do windows, so find out

ahead what is and is not included in the basic cleaning service. Polishing silver and doing laundry are likely extra.

■ What supplies do you need to stock? If the cleaners bring their own products, find out if any are toxic, particularly if you have pets and children.

■ When hiring a service, get the names of the employee(s) who will be cleaning your house. If you are going to have regular service, find out if the same people will come every time.

■ Do you need to be home while the cleaners are working? If you must supply a key, are there any safeguards to keep it from falling into the wrong hands?

■ Does the service have a breakage/damage policy? Ask for proof of liability insurance. Is the service bonded? If so, get a copy of the bond.

■ To be really thorough, call your better business bureau and ask if there are complaints against the company. One complaint may not mean anything, but several should be a warning signal.

SERVICE CONTRACTS

When you contract with an oil or gas company to deliver heating fuel, the provider will likely offer you a service contract when you are discussing terms. A service contract usually consists of two parts. The first involves an inspection and evaluation of your furnace or boiler, which may result in recommendations for upgrades or adjustments for efficiency. The second part of the contract addresses service. For example, your contract may cover you for unlimited service, including emergency repairs and refills, at any time of day or night (24 hours) and holidays. Some contracts cover part replacement only; some cover both parts and labor. Other variables include postage for shipping parts and additional charges for off-hours house calls. Check before you buy.

Usually, there is an option to change the type of service or coverage that you have, and it's not a bad idea to revisit the issue at this time of year. Why? For one thing, you're most aware of your particular fuel needs and problems in the dead of winter. For another, many companies offer you a chance to sign on with them ahead of time for fuel at a fixed rate per gallon, or for a fixed amount of fuel. Oil and gas retailers typically buy supplies six months in advance of the season, and such a commitment from customers allows them to keep costs down. If the winter is warm, the retailer may come out ahead; but if it's cold, or if fuel prices rise, you will likely save money because you won't be obligated to pay more than the amount you agreed on. Usually this option is offered during the summer, after one heating season is over and before the next one starts. Now, however, is the time to calculate how much fuel you are using and how much you are being billed, so that you can make an intelligent decision when the time comes.

DEMYSTIFYING YOUR ELECTRICAL SYSTEM

Unless you are a licensed electrician, all you really need to know about the secret life of your electrical system is how to identify and use the fuse or circuit-breaker box that controls the safe flow of electricity throughout your home. Both do the same job: A fuse box does it with fuses, and a circuit-breaker box does it with switches. Which type do you have? You can tell by quick observation. First, find the box (usually located in a basement or utility room). Open the door: If you see a panel of switches, you have a breaker box; a panel of flat-topped glass knobs screwed into sockets means you have a fuse box.

Fuse boxes are the older system; most newer houses have circuit-breaker boxes. Fuses are fine, but circuit breakers are generally considered safer (you don't have to do any unscrewing) and more dependable. Both systems are designed to cut off the juice to a particular electrical circuit under certain circumstances. When a surge or short occurs, for example, the circuit-breaker switches are automatically "tripped," or shut off, flipping to the off position. Similarly, fuses are designed to "blow," or burn out, from the high heat created when too much current is pulled through them by a short or overload.

WE WILL WIRE YOUR HOUSE

$17.95

for FIVE rooms on the same floor, 12 months to pay

12th & Locust.

UNION ELECTRIC LIGHT AND POWER SERVICE

Get our wiring proposition on "already built" houses

(A flat metal bar or wire just under the glass will melt at a certain temperature.)

When a circuit breaker trips or a fuse blows, it's doing what it's supposed to do. If either happens, you'll know because the fixtures and outlets powered by that circuit won't work. A main fuse (usually a double fuse), located at the top of the fuse-box panel, or a main circuit breaker (a bigger switch at the top, usually labeled) protects the entire electrical system from overloads or shorts. When the main fuse blows or the main breaker trips, all circuits go out and you are completely in the dark.

It's easy to reset the circuit when a circuit-breaker is tripped; just switch it back to the "on" position. When a fuse blows, it turns black or brown from the heat and is out for good, so it must be replaced. To change a blown fuse, unscrew it and replace it with another fuse of the same rating (marked 15 amps, 20 amps, etc.). Fuses can be purchased in a hardware store or electrical supply house. Replacing a main fuse is more complicated because some mains are enclosed in a plastic pull box. You can see a wire bail handle to pull out; when you pull it, the fuse comes with it. For this operation you should use rubber gloves and a fuse puller, or call a professional.

If you overloaded the circuit in question—by running an air-conditioner, microwave, and hair dryer simultaneously, say—you should do some unplugging. If you make adjustments and the breaker trips or a fuse blows again, there is a problem with the circuit and further checking and unplugging is in order. If you can't solve the problem by process of elimination, call a professional. (You definitely want to get an electrician if a short has been caused by something dangerous, like a bad switch.)

The entire resetting process is much easier if your circuits or fuses are labeled. To identify them, shut off one circuit at a time (flip the switch or remove the fuse), note what stops working, and label accordingly. You can also ask your electrician to do this for you.

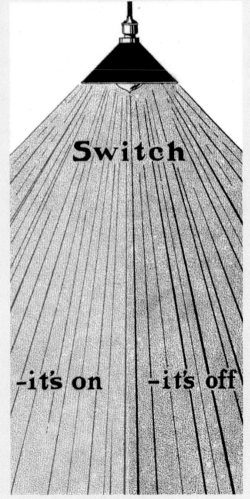

OUTSIDE

■ **Check bulbs in outdoor fixtures to be sure they haven't burned out.** Lightbulbs don't last nearly as long in the cold as they do indoors. Consider using halogen bulbs, which yield more light for less energy. These give off a pure white light, last longer than incandescent bulbs, and are more efficient.

■ **Remove any debris that may have collected outside the clothes drier vent.** Be sure nothing, including ice or snow, has lodged in or near the vent and that the flapper is free and operating. If it gets stuck open, rodents and other critters can migrate inside. To be sure it works smoothly, lubricate it with silicone spray.

TIP Do Houses Come with Warranties? Some builders offer warranties for new homes, but a house that has been previously owned does not come with one. Ask your real estate agent to obtain a "total disclosure" from the seller (required by law in some states). This must include such information as the age of the roof and heating system, a history of fire and other damage, and problems with termites. Because uncovering potential problems can be a good bargaining chip, a disclosure statement serves the buyer, but it also reminds owners of the value of maintaining a house well.

DECK,
PORCH,
AND
*P*ATIO

■ **Use your gas grill.** Cold weather is good for grilling with gas. Just remember to check your fuel tank more often because the grill runs on gases that evaporate from the propane rather than on the fuel itself. Less gas is produced when the fuel is cold, and the propane doesn't burn as efficiently.

■ **Store propane tanks safely.** Don't store the propane tanks for your grill inside your home, especially near the boiler or furnace. Even in cold weather, keep them outside, away from any source of heat or flame. Unlike natural gas, propane is heavier than air. Because it diffuses more slowly than natural gas, you may not smell the propane. An unnoticed leaky can is not something you want inside. A little soapy solution rubbed around the fittings and valve will create bubbles if there's a leak. If the tank is leaking, return it immediately to the store where you bought it.

■ **Identify areas that need more lighting in the dark of winter.** Add light fixtures or install higher-wattage bulbs, but be careful not to use a bulb with more wattage than the fixture can handle. If the maximum wattage is not indicated on the fixture, use common sense. A small fixture is not designed to withstand the heat of a 200-watt bulb. When in doubt use a low-watt bulb (40–60 watts) until you can consult an electrician.

 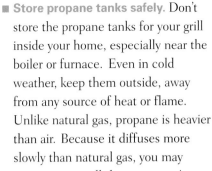

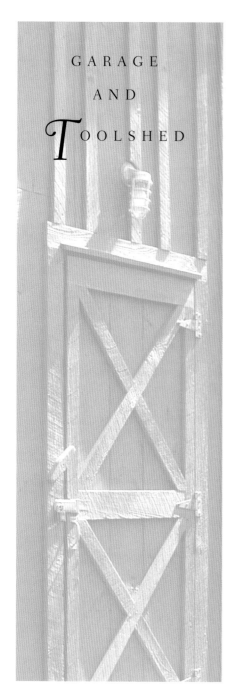

GARAGE AND *T*OOLSHED

■ **Give your tools a once-over.**
Sharpen any dull blades and take inventory to see what you may need for upcoming spring projects.

■ **Organize your potting bench.**
Recycle those plastic pots from last season's bedding plants that you are never going to use. If you take them to your local garden center, they'll be put to good use. Clean and sanitize clay and other pots and planters that you are saving for another summer; rinse them with a bleach-and-water solution to kill bacteria and mildew. Sort through your garden paraphernalia, and store stakes and peony rings where you can get them when you want them.

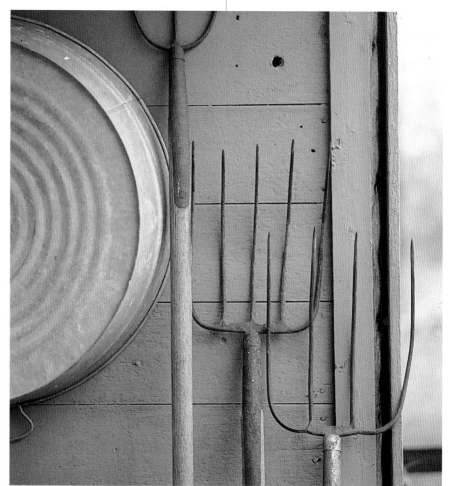

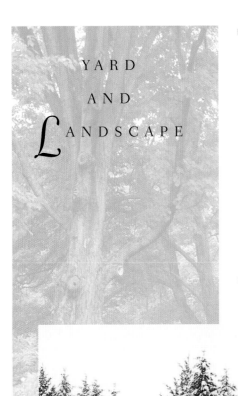

YARD AND *L*ANDSCAPE

■ **Check driveway and other markers** (fuel tank, for example) to make sure they are still clearly visible. By midwinter, I find half of my driveway markers have been knocked over by the plow or submerged under the piles of snow that accumulate at the end of the drive after each plowing. The fewer the markers, the greater the chance that the plow or another vehicle will trespass onto your lawn during the next pass.

■ **Continue your yard and garden survey.** Make clean pruning cuts to trim broken twigs and branches from trees and shrubs to prevent pest infestation when the weather gets warmer. If you notice that plants are heaving, add straw or more evergreens as mulch.

■ **Check the edges of steps, walkways, and your driveway for winter damage.** The sand distributed by snowplows is often mixed with a heavy dose of salt. If this mixture is migrating onto your grass or garden beds, protect them with straw mulch. Do the same for any areas vulnerable to municipal sidewalk salting, and wherever you can't control the content of the de-icer. Whenever you apply a melting agent yourself, try to stay away from salt, which may pit concrete, stone pavers, and bricks; it also may damage mortar joints, and stain wood. Use a commercial nonsalt melting agent or cat litter.

■ **Stay off frozen grass**. As you walk around your property during the winter, remember that grass is particularly vulnerable to foot traffic when the ground is frozen. Stick to paths and stairs as much as possible.

■ **Prune fruit trees**. In northern climates, February is the time to trim apple and pear trees because they are dormant now. Cut off branches that are low on the trunk and trim the weakest branches to strengthen the healthier ones.

■ **Clean your birdhouses**. Check bluebird boxes and any other man-made condos for our feathered friends for traces of old nests. Last year's nesting materials should be removed before unwelcome pests start to infest. Rinse the birdhouses thoroughly with plain hot water.

INSIDE

- Freshen your linens.
- Wash floors.
- Stock up on basic household cleansers.
- Force spring branches for bouquets.
- Test your water.
- Test your water main.

OUTSIDE

- Survey metal railings for deterioration.
- Check wood shingles and roof shakes for mold.
- Inspect the exterior masonry or cladding of your house for storm damage.

DECK, PORCH, AND PATIO

- Maintain your grill.
- Inspect built-in planters.
- Assess outdoor outlet capabilities.
- Check for dry rot.

GARAGE AND TOOLSHED

- Prep your tools and lawn equipment.
- Check the air in the tires of your mower and wheelbarrows.

YARD AND LANDSCAPE

- Begin organizing spring yard and garden help.
- Survey fences and stone walls for problems.
- Top-dress garden beds.
- Fertilize early bulb plants.
- Check shrubs for snow buildup.
- Pick up twigs, branches, and other deadfall.
- Clean up gravel deposited during snow plowing.

March

According to an old saying, New England's calendar year contains nine months of winter, two months of summer, and one month of poor sledding. Anyone who lives in milder climes is already enjoying the blooms of dogwood, azaleas, and other harbingers of the new season; even up north, March offers the hope that spring exists. Take advantage of the first mild days to air out your house by throwing open your basement doors and attic windows.

INSIDE

- **Freshen your linens.** Take on some early spring cleaning: Collect pillows, comforters, and featherbeds and treat them to a good airing and fluffing. Launder mattress covers and cotton shower curtains in hot water. On a warm day line dry your sheets.

- **Wash floors.** This should be a regular chore throughout the snow and mud season. Use a product specified for the type of flooring you have, be it wood, vinyl, rubber tile, cork, marble, or ceramic or quarry tile. Check to see if the flooring manufacturer recommends a specific cleanser (another reason to save your manuals and warranties) or a polish to add extra shine. When polish or wax builds up after six to eight coats, it should be stripped before you repolish. Try using a solution of ½ cup powdered floor cleanser or 2 cups ammonia in a gallon of cool water. Scrub the flooring with very fine steel wool and rinse and dry thoroughly; then apply fresh polish.

  If they are well sealed or varnished with polyurethane, wood floors can be cleaned safely with a product specified for this purpose or with a vinegar-and-water solution; but they should always be dried immediately and thoroughly. Oiled wood floors should be reoiled annually. Clean them with Murphy Oil Soap and reoil, using a solution of equal parts turpentine and boiled (not raw) linseed oil (See "Caring for Wood Paneling," January). You can also use tung oil, but do not use a product specified for varnished floors. If you're not sure what might or might not work, spot test with the cleaning solution first.

- **Stock up on basic household cleansers.** These include ammonia, bleach, window and floor cleanser, and at least one good all-purpose product. Baking soda and vinegar are handy as well. Replace your vacuum cleaner bag.

- **Force spring branches for bouquets.** Coax cut branches of forsythia, lilacs, and fruit trees into bloom by putting the stems in water (crush the ends first). The trick is to spritz the branches frequently with a mister.

- **Test your water.** It's a good idea to test well water every year or two, especially if there has been activity in the vicinity, such as repairs to a septic system, excavation, blasting, or road or drainage work. Well water comes from an aquifer deep in the ground, so minor changes or disturbances probably won't affect it. All aquifers, however, are fed by seeping water (the seeping is part of the purifying process). And because water seeps into the ground from numerous sources, it is best to be cautious. Early spring is a good time to check for groundwater problems. Lead, radon, and nitrate pose health hazards; other infiltrators, like calcium, sulfur, and iron, can discolor your water or give it an unpleasant smell, but they are not dangerous.

Any commercial testing company will check water for bacteria and other contaminants. The company will usually test your water's hardness gratis, then suggest a bacteria test, for which there is a charge. Go for it; if something is wrong, you will want to know.

If you have your own well, call the health department in your area to see if testing is warranted. If you don't have a private well, ask your water company for a copy of its most recent analysis. You can also ask the water company, health department, or cooperative extension agency to refer you to a reliable testing agency, or check the Yellow Pages under "Laboratories—Testing." I don't recommend relying on a home-testing kit.

- **Test your water main.** Turn it off, then turn it on again. It's a good idea to do this periodically throughout the year to make sure the valve isn't difficult to operate. You can usually use an adjustable crescent wrench, but consider investing in a special T-shaped water-main wrench made to fit over the lug on the water valve. Either tool should be on hand in case of a water emergency.

DEMYSTIFYING YOUR WATER SYSTEM

D o you know where (or what) your water main is? This is a simple but important question, and I am constantly surprised at how few homeowners know the answer.

The main is the primary pipe that supplies your home with water—from either a public municipal water supply or your private well. The water main is equipped with a shutoff valve, which you should know how to operate in case of an emergency—a leak or a frozen pipe—that requires a temporary shutdown of your water supply to remedy. The valve is usually located where the water line enters the house (typically the basement or crawl space). Ask your plumber to show you how it works.

Turning off the water main is not dangerous, but there are related considerations. A typical hot water heater or boiler, for example, is designed to shut off automatically if the water level gets too low. In the course of ordinary usage, such appliances replenish their own water supplies. However, if the water main is turned off for more than a few days, the boiler will not be able to refill adequately and will eventually shut off. If the situation is so dire that you must turn your water off for a protracted period, you probably are not planning to stay home while you get the problem fixed; but you should still know that your boiler might shut off. (To prevent this, your plumber would install a temporary water bypass.) If the main is turned off briefly (a few hours or a day or two), there is not much to worry about. Be aware, though, that certain appliances, like automatic ice makers, may need refilling after the main has been turned back on. Check the manufacturer's recommendations.

To get into your home's plumbing system, well water is usually sent by a submersible pump (located near the well bottom) to a pressure tank in or near the house. As the name implies, this keeps the water pressurized (which is why water immediately flows when you turn on a faucet). Town water, on the other hand, is pressurized at the water plant and may be directed to your house by gravity (as from a water tower), rather than by a pump. If you have public water, your supply is metered, in much the same way your electricity is. The water meter is usually inside the house, typically in the basement or a utility closet. Some municipalities have remote readers attached to the meter so it can be read from outside the house.

Anyone who has a private well knows that one of the potential problems is hard water, the term for water that contains high levels of calcium, iron, magnesium, and a few other elements. These eventually settle and can clog pipes, water heaters, and other appliances, such as dishwashers and washing machines, as well as leaving behind stains and bathroom scum.

The answer to hard water is a water-softening system. A water softener works by filtering your water through a medium, a loose material charged to attract the minerals from the water, such as salt. The medium is recharged on a regular timer, and you have to refill the softener with salt periodically. Softened water contains a safe level of salt, and does not taste saltier, because the salt is used only to temper the medium and enable the softener to do its work. However, don't use softened water in your garden—the salt is not safe for plants. Your outdoor faucets should be on a separate line.

Although town water supplies are required to meet EPA standards, it doesn't hurt to filter your tap water, particularly if you use well water. Filtering can improve taste, reduce odors, and lower existing levels of chlorine, lead, and waterborne microorganisms such as cryptosporidium, a parasite that can cause disease. Some faucet filters contain a carbon filter; others use a reverse osmosis filtration system that delivers filtered water via a separate tap. Refrigerators also come with filtered on-door dispensers.

TIP Water Leaks The water meters that measure water consumption from municipal supplies can also be used to detect leaks. To test for a leak, take a reading, then turn off all water-related fixtures in your house, including appliances like ice machines, and let everything rest for a few hours. Take a second reading; if it has changed, a leak is likely.

10 USES FOR VINEGAR

1. Spray full strength to kill weeds and unwanted grass on walks and driveways.

2. Apply a solution of equal parts vinegar and water around doors, baseboards, appliances, and cupboards to repel ants.

3. Deodorize a sink or shower drain by pouring a cup of vinegar down it. Let it stand for half an hour, then flush the drain thoroughly with water. To unclog a drain, put in a handful of baking soda followed by 1/2 cup vinegar, then rinse with hot water.

4. Clean cutting boards with full-strength vinegar.

5. Add a tablespoon of vinegar to hot, soapy water to cut grease on pots and pans; use it undiluted to clean deposits in your coffeemaker.

6. Remove stains in pots by boiling a solution of 3 tablespoons vinegar to 1 pint water.

7. Soak bolts and hinges in full-strength vinegar to dissolve rust.

8. To freshen the washing machine, pour a cup of vinegar into the clothes basin and run though a regular cycle (without clothes) to dissolve detergent residue.

9. Remove decals by brushing with vinegar.

10. To freshen cut flowers, put them in a solution of 1 quart water to 2 tablespoons vinegar and 1 teaspoon sugar.

OUTSIDE

■ **Survey metal railings for deterioration.** In particular, check the areas where the metal comes in contact with wet ground for signs of rusting and corrosion. Minor problems can be treated on a dry day: Scrape off flaking and rusting paint with a wire brush and prime and retouch with rust-inhibiting paint products.

■ **Check wood shingles and roof shakes for mold.** You can kill the mold and clean the shingles in one fell swoop with a solution of chlorine bleach and water. If you don't remove the mold, the shingles can't dry out thoroughly, and they'll eventually rot. For big jobs, consider using a pressure washer. Also try to determine what is causing the mold. You may need to improve air circulation by cutting back bushes or trees that are near the shingles.

■ **Inspect the exterior masonry or cladding of your house for storm damage,** especially under eaves and near leaders (downspouts), which can freeze and break. Examine the foundation from top to bottom for masonry cracks.

 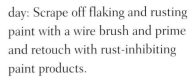

DECK,

PORCH,

AND

*P*ATIO

■ **Maintain your grill.** Empty a charcoal grill of ash regularly, keep the vents clear, and clean the rack each time you use it. If you haven't used your gas grill for several months, install a new fuel can. Check the lines and fittings for leaks and corrosion, to avoid "back blow" (an exploding gas buildup) when lighting; it can singe your hair and eyebrows. When you ignite the grill, make sure the lid is wide open, and don't turn on the gas until you are ready to light.

■ **Inspect built-in planters.** If you haven't been emptying them of snow and ice, do so now. Make any necessary repairs.

■ **Assess outdoor outlet capabilities.** You'll want to be sure that outdoor outlets and circuits meet your lighting and other needs—music systems, laptop computer, electric cooktop, or rotisserie. Outdoor outlets should be housed in weatherproof boxes with spring-loaded covers to keep rain and moisture out; they should be fitted with a ground-fault circuit interrupter (GFCI) to protect against short-circuiting mishaps.

■ **Check for dry rot.** Dry rot is just what it sounds like: a powdery rot that quite literally crumbles away in your hand. Although the rot looks and feels dry, the condition is actually caused by a fungus that thrives on dampness—which is why you want to keep a wood porch or deck sealed or painted properly (see "Check decking for winter damage," April). You should also trim nearby shrubbery so that air can circulate. You can often detect dry rot early because the affected wood turns brown or gray-white and may emit a musty odor before reaching the rotting, powdery stage. (Wear a face mask when you are making your survey because dry rot can aggravate allergies.) The fungus can go dormant if the moisture dries up or the air temperature drops below 40°F, but it will become active again as soon as conditions are favorable for new growth. The best solution is to replace the affected wood and treat any areas that might become infected with a good wood preservative. And try to reverse the conditions (dampness, for example) that are causing the dry rot. When using a wood preservative, wear goggles and gloves because these substances contain toxic ingredients such as copper and zinc salt compounds. Remember that anything strong enough to kill bugs and fungus can't be good for us either.

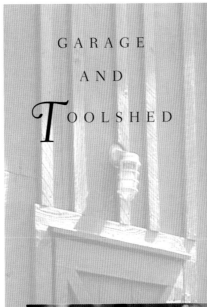

GARAGE
AND
*T*OOLSHED

■ **Prep your tools and lawn equipment.** You'll want to have all your tools ready to use on the first nice day, so be sure they are clean and sharp. If you've stored your lawn mower, take it out now and give it a test start. Make sure you have all the accessories you'll need, such as a replacement cord for your weed whacker.

■ **Check the air in the tires of your mower and wheelbarrows.** If the tires are low or flat, pump them up with a bicycle pump. Fill gas cans and check oil levels.

YARD
AND
*L*ANDSCAPE

■ **Begin organizing spring yard and garden help.** If you use a professional maintenance staff for your pool or automatic sprinkler system, make a date to check systems. Line up your help now; good, reliable yard workers get booked very early.

■ **Survey fences and stone walls for problems.** Check the concrete footings of wooden fence posts to make sure they have not cracked during the freeze-thaw cycle. Examine stone walls for stones loosened or heaved by frost and replace them as necessary.

■ **Top-dress garden beds.** Feeding your beds builds up the nitrogen, phosphorus, and potassium content of the soil. Use well-rotted organic manure that has been composted or "resting" in a

manure heap for at least a year because the ammonia in fresh manure is harmful to plants and new growth.

- **Fertilize early bulb plants.** If you did not feed plants in the fall, do it now. Use a fertilizer with a balanced pH factor; if you use one with a high nitrogen content, you'll feed the leaves instead of nourishing the blossoms.

- **Check shrubs for snow buildup.** The heavy, wet snow of late-winter storms can pose a real threat, particularly when new growth is just beginning to sprout. Brush snow off flat-topped hedges as soon as it starts to accumulate.

- **Pick up twigs, branches, and other deadfall.** The more you clean up now, the less you'll have to do before your first mowing. Rake up the detritus from last year's autumn leaf crop.

- **Clean up gravel deposited during snow plowing.** Gravel and dirt deposits will kill grass and inhibit new growth, so keep your lawn clear. If the area is small, try raking. Otherwise, see if your plow operator or landscape worker can clear the gravel away with a mechanical brush made for this purpose; it's much more effective than raking.

NATURAL FERTILIZERS

If you are about to clean out your fireplace or woodstove, consider saving the ashes. Dry wood ash makes a fine fertilizer for soil in need of alkaline content, and it is also great to throw on the compost pile because the ash remains rich in the minerals that were in the wood before it burned. Among these are potassium and phosphorus, which benefit garden soil and help prevent plant disease. Potassium is good for the stems of plants, and phosphorus is important for root, seed, and fruit development; it also nourishes root vegetables and flower bulbs as they grow.

Remember that embers can smolder for long periods of time, so be sure that all coals are totally burned out and cool. When preparing your garden beds in the spring (or putting them to bed in the fall), apply the fully cooled ashes with your back to the wind, sprinkling them on the soil and working them in with a fork or trowel. As you turn over the soil, toss in a handful each of the ash, with rotted organic manure (or commercial fertilizer), and moistened peat moss over each four to five cubic feet.

STONE WALLS

It is often said that the primary crop harvested by early New England farmers was rocks. If the thousands of stone walls crisscrossing the region are any measure, there's truth in the saying. The notoriously stony New England landscape, produced by the last glacial retreat (about 7,000 years ago), made tough going for early settlers and their plows. As they prepared fields for planting, farmers saved the shale, slate, schist, and limestone they cleared and built walls to fence in animals and mark property boundaries. Rather than cutting or chiseling the stones, the farmers simply sorted them according to size and shape and put them to the most logical use: Those with two flat faces meeting at a right angle, for example, made good cornerstones, while the broad, flat ones served as capstones to span the top of the wall.

Thousands of these stone walls remain, often snaking down into gullies and up steep hillsides. The new woods that have grown up over the past 50 or 60 years can make it hard to imagine that such terrain was ever farmed, but virtually any place where an old stone wall still exists was once cleared and used for crops or grazing. That so many stone walls still survive may seem remarkable because they were traditionally dry-laid, or built without mortar. Dry-laid walls, however, actually last longer than those built with mortar because the stones are free to move and settle, and they permit water to drain naturally through the rocks.

SPRING

Once they get hooked on a particular task, most people who enjoy working on projects around the house can't stop thinking about it. Anyone who has ever experienced the compulsion to plant the season's first annuals or paint the porch floor knows that the urge can border on obsession. My addiction is tools. Though I admit that there is no time of year when holding a well-made tool in my hand doesn't give me pleasure, spring always finds me adding something new to my collection. Part of the reason is that the projects that usually need doing in the spring demand your attention at a time of year when you want to be doing them. You may not feel the same way about it in the dead of January or the dog days of August—but who in their right mind wouldn't want to head for the hardware store on the first nice day in April?

I am privileged to own the same box of tools that my grandfather used when he began his working days, at the end of the 1800s, as a carpenter and craftsman in upstate New York. As was then the custom, not only was he able to put up an entire building with what now seems limited equipment—handsaw, plane, hammer, ruler, chisel, plumb bob, clapboard hook—but he also made most of his tools (or at least the handles) himself.

Even if I didn't think of my grandfather every time I held one of his planes or homemade mallets in my palm, I couldn't pick up any tool without remembering who taught me how to use it and when. I regard tools as an extension of both hand and mind. You can learn how to use one in an hour and still spend a lifetime developing the skill to get it to do what you want. But that learning process—the maturing of the mind-to-tool connection—is what's so exhilarating. At some point you reach a threshold and begin to realize that what's making it all work has less to do with mastering technical skill than with having acquired a natural feel for both tool and process. Then you're there.

That said, my message for this time of year is a simple one. When you're gearing up for spring cleaning, remember your toolbox. If you don't have a good selection of tools, let the season and whatever tasks that come with it inspire you to compile one. If you have a toolbox, consider it your duty to add at least one great new tool to it—or take advantage of spring tag sales to start a collection of antiques.

THINGS TO DO IN APRIL

INSIDE

- Adjust timers for daylight saving time.
- Wash your windows.
- Make sure major appliances are sitting level.
- Prepare closets and chests for storing winter clothes and linens.
- Protect stored winter items with insect repellents.
- Change the batteries in your smoke detectors.
- Start kitchen herbs inside for transplanting later in May.

OUTSIDE

- Climb a ladder and survey your roof.
- Examine exterior wiring.
- Check windows.
- Replace storm windows with screens.

DECK, PORCH, AND PATIO

- Check decking for winter damage.
- Clean surfaces.
- Survey parts of the deck or porch near garden beds or planters.

GARAGE AND TOOLSHED

- Sweep out the garage or vacuum with a shop vacuum.
- Check your lawn maintenance equipment.
- Bring your garden hoses out of storage.
- Get out the grill and make sure it's clean and ready to go.
- Take your garden furniture out of storage.

YARD AND LANDSCAPE

- Make sure outdoor water systems are up and running.
- Examine retaining walls for winter damage.
- Drain birdbaths and other receptacles.
- Start preparing new garden beds.
- Get existing perennial beds ready for the new season.
- Transplant and divide summer- and fall-blooming perennials.
- Check shrubs and trees for winter damage.
- Repair lawn areas.

April

*E*ven in the most temperate regions of the country, April comes as a welcome break from winter doldrums. In my neck of the woods, it has something to do with the subtle greens and yellows of the emerging leaves, the sound of tree frogs, and the incurable urge I always have to get outdoors and crank up the tractor. There's something in the air, and along with it comes the universal impulse to tackle spring cleaning, both inside and outside the house.

*I*NSIDE

■ **Adjust timers for daylight saving time.** Spring ahead and fall back. The idea of setting clocks ahead an hour in the spring, then reverting back to standard time in the fall, dates at least as far back as the 1700s, when Benjamin Franklin (serving as U.S. minister to France) recommended earlier opening and closing times for shops to save on lighting costs. We continue the practice now primarily to extend daylight hours for recreation and to conserve energy. These days, that means we set in April the increasing number of household gadgets that run on timers, then reset them in October. Remember to check any timers regulating the thermostats on your heating system (some can be complicated, so read the manual). You will also need to reset the timers on indoor and outdoor lights (these are usually remote, and found in the garage, utility room, or basement).

■ **Wash your windows.** Early spring is a good time to take on this chore: It will literally improve your outlook on the world. Satisfy the impulse to clean the haze and grime left behind by winter storms by tackling the job while the weather is still cool; if you wash windows on hot, sunny days, the soap solution can dry before you get it off, causing filmy streaks. Start indoors before you've installed your screens, then finish the job outside on a dry day.

Clean one pane at a time, working from the top down with a

sponge: Use a good commercial spray cleaner or make your own solution (try 4 tablespoons ammonia to a gallon of water or equal parts vinegar and water). Dry with a clean lint-free cloth as you go. When using a rubber-bladed squeegee, sweep in one continuous motion back and forth from the top down, catching the dirty water with a cloth on the last swipe to keep it from running down the walls or onto the sill. Remove streaks in a final polishing with a dry cloth reserved for this last step. (Some people swear by a final wipe with crumpled newspaper to remove dried soap film and streaks, but I find that the ink can smear.)

■ **Make sure major appliances are sitting level.** This is important to do at least once annually, and spring is as good a time as any. Dishwashers, washing machines, humidifiers, and air conditioners are designed to run at maximum efficiency when absolutely level. If they go off kilter, which can happen with frequent use, the parts wear out more quickly and might even shake loose when an appliance tips or rattles. Simply use a spirit level to check for "good posture." You can correct minor problems with shims; otherwise, call a professional for help.

■ **Prepare closets and chests for storing winter clothes and linens.** Emptying your closets and vacuuming them thoroughly helps protect against insect infestation (repellents do not kill larvae) and also offers a chance to sort items.

Remember to dry clean or wash winter clothes, blankets, and linens before storing them for the summer in order to rid them of pet hairs, oils, and other substances that attract moths.

■ **Protect stored winter items with insect repellents.** Among the most effective natural moth repellents I know is a cotton sachet filled with cedar chips; tuck a few in your drawers or loop them around the necks of hangers. Cedar hangers

and shoe trees are another idea, or you can try a bundle of bay leaves. Mothballs are another traditional choice, but the distinctive camphor odor tends to permeate fabrics, and the balls are toxic if ingested; they're not a great idea if your household includes children or pets.

In any case, no repellent will work effectively unless the storage area is sealed tightly. Pack your goods in a closet or chest that you won't be opening all the time, or put them away in zip-up garment bags or plastic bins with lids.

■ **Change the batteries in your smoke detectors.** In addition to testing smoke detector batteries regularly, you should change them twice a year without fail. Make one change an automatic part of your regular spring maintenance schedule. If you have a sump pump, its alarm battery should also be changed every spring before the rainy season sets in.

■ **Start kitchen herbs inside for transplanting later in May.** Basil, chives, cilantro, dill, parsley, fennel, lemongrass, and sweet marjoram can all be started relatively easily from seeds. Oregano, rosemary, sage, savory, and tarragon do better if you start them from small plants or cuttings.

CEDAR CLOSETS

Packing away winter clothes and linens and getting out the warm-weather alternatives is one of the more enjoyable aspects of the annual spring cleaning routine because it so clearly marks the arrival of the season. That said, remember that the woolens you are storing make an ideal nesting area for adult moths (and their voracious offspring)— which means that spring storage requires more than merely folding away sweaters and blankets in a closet or bureau without using some kind of repellent.

One of the best and most traditional repellents is cedar. (Remember that distinctive fragrance in your grandmother's linen closet?) In this case the cedar in question is aromatic eastern red cedar, found mainly in the southern Appalachians: As the oils in the milled wood evaporate, they emit a rich odor that is so repellent to moths that the insects will not reproduce in any area permeated by the scent.

Cedar-lined closets first became prevalent in this country in the late 1800s, when built-in closets began to replace freestanding wardrobes. If you own a house with an old cedar closet, you'll find that the natural cedar scent may still be fresh, especially if the door is tight and the closet has been kept clean. When dirt buildup and air infiltration have dulled both the scent and color of the wood, you can revive the cedar by sanding it lightly with a fine-grade sandpaper; this will reopen the pores and release the oils anew. You can also treat the wood with natural cedar oil extract, but you should never apply any kind of varnish or sealer.

If you are installing a new cedar closet, have your builder fill any gaps between the walls, floor, and ceiling before fitting the cedar lining. The door should be tight. If you don't have a true cedar closet, it is possible to convert an ordinary one by using the cedar lining products, including pure cedar wood and aromatic cedar flake board, sold at home building stores. Make sure it is aromatic eastern red cedar rather than a western variety.

PREPARING FOR FIRE EMERGENCIES

The two most important types of safety equipment required for all households are smoke detectors (also called smoke alarms) and fire extinguishers. Both should be checked constantly to make sure they are working properly.

Smoke detectors: By sounding a piercing alarm, smoke detectors buy you precious time in the event of fire. There are two basic kinds: battery-operated and AC-powered units. Battery-operated detectors are easy to install, but are less reliable than the electric AC units because the batteries can run out or go bad. AC units require an electrician for installation, but be sure there is still a battery backup in case of a power outage or electrical fire.

Whatever the choice, you should have at least one smoke detector installed on the ceiling of each level of your home, one in the kitchen, and one outside every bedroom door (check local electrical codes). You should also have a heat or smoke detector installed in or near the boiler or furnace area. Battery models are designed to emit a series of bleeps when the juice is low and contain a light to indicate they are functioning, but either can be unreliable. Test the battery once a month yourself. Climb a ladder or use a broomstick to press the test button. If the battery is okay, the alarm will sound; no noise means a dead battery, so you should change it immediately.

To make sure either type of smoke detector is actually functioning, hold a smoking candle end or match under it. If the alarm doesn't sound, the unit needs replacing.

Fire extinguishers: Keep a separate unit in the kitchen, basement, and garage, and at least one elsewhere on each level of the house. Common wisdom dictates one pressure-gauge extinguisher per 600 square feet. These should be placed in plain view. Make sure every family member knows where all the extinguishers are. I even keep one in our coat closet because I know everyone sees it whenever they open the door.

There are four basic extinguisher types, rated A, B, C, and ABC. The type A fire extinguisher is designed to put out fires involving normal household combustibles, such as paper, plastic, and wood. Type B extinguishers are for more highly volatile substances like gas and fuel oil, and Type C are for electrical fires. The ABC-rated extinguisher is an all-in-one model. For most households, ABC is the recommended rating. You don't, for example, want to use a C extinguisher on a paper fire—but you won't have time to think about it when you are grabbing the extinguisher in an emergency.

Each month, check the pressure gauge in every extinguisher to make sure it is charged. If the pressure is low, you need to recharge (see manufacturer's instructions) or replace it. In case of fire, pull the pin, aim at the base of the fire, and squeeze the handle. Still aiming at the base of the fire, sweep the spray from side to side, working from front to back. If you cannot put out the fire, get everyone out of the house immediately and call 911 from another location.

OUTSIDE

■ **Climb a ladder and survey your roof** carefully for any damage left by winter storms and spring rains. Ice chunks and the constant freeze-thaw process can lift and warp shingles and chip or dislodge the bricks in chimneys. While you're up there, check all the gutters and the flashings around the chimney bases, dormers, and the like, to make sure they haven't been damaged or pulled away in a storm. Keep an eye out for popped-up nails as well.

■ **Examine exterior wiring.** Look at the phone and electric wire connections to make sure nothing has pulled loose. Then run your eye along the length of the wires, looking above for loose or hanging tree limbs that might fall and catch or pull down a wire. If you see such a hazard, make sure you notify the appropriate utility company.

■ **Check windows to be sure that frames and sills have not splintered or pulled away from the wall.** You can also probe with a sharp knife to detect rot or insect damage.

■ **Replace storm windows with screens.** Remove your storm windows (or adjust sliding models by sliding the storms up and screens down) before completing your exterior window washing. If you are installing separate screens, now is the time to repair any damage that occurred when you took them out of storage. Wash with a hose, and patch any snags or tears.

PREVENTING FLOOD DAMAGE

These days you are unlikely to buy a house without being warned of the potential danger of flooding in coastal or riverine areas. For one thing, most mortgage companies require that you purchase flood insurance if your house is in a danger area. But you may not know that seemingly innocent streams and drainage ditches can overflow and cause a flash flood in a heavy rainstorm.

To protect against water damage, make sure that all areas around the foundation of your house are graded to direct ground water away from the structure; even the slightest incline toward your home can cause water to seep. Any exposed parts of the foundation can be waterproofed with a masonry paint or silicone spray designed for this purpose.

I also recommend that anyone living in wetland or flood-prone areas install a sump pump in their basement. Sump pumps, usually placed in the lowest part of the basement (called the sump), are designed to turn on automatically by means of a float-activated switch, if and when the area begins filling with water. You can also install an inexpensive battery-operated alarm fitted with a moisture sensor on the floor next to the pump. This will sound when the sensor gets wet, alerting you when water starts collecting.

There are two basic types of electric sump pump: upright and submersible. In an upright, or pedestal, model, the motor sits atop the pump so that it doesn't get wet. The base is placed in the bottom of the sump, and a self-activating ball-float switch starts the motor. Submersible sump pumps are designed as in-ground models and are intended to work underwater. These may have a ball float connected to an internal pressure switch or a sealed, adjustable mercury-activated switch, which is generally more reliable than a pressure switch. A third type of sump pump is water-activated. Running off the water pressure of your plumbing system, it pumps more slowly than an electric pump. On the other hand, it keeps running even if the electricity goes out, which is often the case during severe storms.

Whatever the type of pump, the water should be discharged at least 20 feet away from the house so that it drains away from the foundation. It should not be directed onto a neighbor's property, into window wells, or into a septic-system leaching field. Most sump pumps come with directions and installation instructions. If you don't feel up to the job, call a plumber. Any type of pump should have a check valve on the water outlet pipe to prevent water from flowing back into the sump when the pump shuts off. Repeated flow-back action can cause the pump to turn on and off too often and shorten its life.

If your sump pump has not been activated in more than two months, test it. To do so, slowly pour about five gallons of water into the sump. Watch the action of the on/off switch and listen to the pump, making it turn on and off at least twice. If it doesn't turn on or appear to be running smoothly, have it checked by a professional.

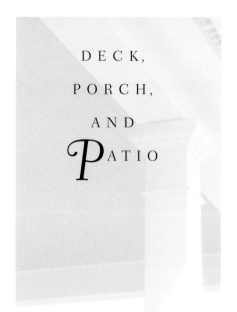

DECK, PORCH, AND *P*ATIO

■ **Check decking for winter damage.** Look for warped or rotted boards and loose nails and screws. Constant exposure to the elements may mean your deck needs resealing as often as once a year to protect it from UV degradation and moisture.

If the finish has faded or worn off, now is the time to reseal, before hot weather sets in. You can test the need for resealing by pouring a glass of water directly on a dry area of decking. If the water beads, the existing finish is still doing its job. If the decking sops up the water quickly and turns dark, you need to reseal. A variety of stains, oils, and

sealers are available for this specific purpose. (Paint is not typically recommended for decking because the constantly exposed surface tends to split and bubble.) Sealing should be done on a dry, windless day, especially when you are using a spray-on product.

■ **Clean surfaces.** Even if you don't need to reseal your deck, it is due for a spring cleaning to remove grime, pollen, fungus, moss, and mildew. Commercial deck cleansers and restorative products are made for this purpose. A heavy-duty cleaning job may require a pressure washer, which can be rented from hardware stores. An alternative is to scrub with a cleaning formula made with a cup of powdered laundry detergent added to a gallon of hot water; add a ½ cup of liquid chlorine bleach to kill moss or mildew.

■ **Survey any part of the deck or porch that comes in contact with garden beds or planters.** Check to make sure that moist dirt doesn't pile up against the wood decking, which can happen as mulching builds up the level of a flower bed. Constant contact with wet dirt can cause rot and insect infestation, so you'll want to shovel away any extra soil or mulch that touches wood surfaces.

GARAGE AND *T*OOLSHED

■ **Sweep out the garage or vacuum with a shop vacuum.** It's important to remove the surprising amounts of dirt that migrate in on your tires from driveways and roads where snowplows have deposited salt and sand.

■ **Check your lawn maintenance equipment** to make sure everything is operating properly. Fill your lawn mower with gas, take it outside, and try starting it, so you know everything is in working order well before you set out for your first mowing. Do the same with your lawn tractor if you have one.

■ **Bring your garden hoses out of storage.** Check for cracks and leaks, particularly if they have been stored in unheated toolsheds. Examine the rubber or plastic washers at the connectors as well.

■ **Get out the grill and make sure it's clean and ready to go.** If your gas grill has sat unused over the winter, carefully check the jets for clogging and obstructions, including insect and rodent nests. If one jet lights but the other clogs, gas buildup on the clogged side can cause an explosive combustion when the gas finally lights.

■ **Take your garden furniture out of storage.** The occasional balmy April day may mean you'll want to use it! No matter how well you cleaned and covered your lawn furniture before winter storage, you'll probably need to go over it with a damp sponge and a dry, clean cloth to remove storage dust.

TOOLBOX ESSENTIALS

*T*he first element of a tool collection is the box. Choose one with several compartments or lift-out trays so you can organize items and find them quickly. Although I prefer metal (a more traditional choice), you'll find a far bigger selection of boxes in plastic. Actually, the plastic is more durable because it won't dent or rust. As you accumulate tools over time, you'll likely end up with two or three boxes. (I probably have more than a hundred hammers, and that's not even counting my other tools!) Pegboard storage is a good idea for larger items, like handsaws, that won't fit in your box.

When purchasing a tool, hold it in your hand and check the feel: Do the handle and weight feel comfortable? You should also be sure that you are buying the right tool for the right job. If you don't know, investigate and ask for help from the sales staff. Almost all tools come in various sizes and weights. Describe the task you're tackling and make sure that the tool is the right type and size to do the job safely.

Most simple do-it-yourself household and yard tasks require one or more of these basic tools:

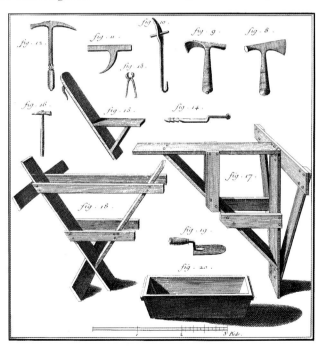

Carpenter's hammer: For general use I recommend a medium-size hammer (16 to 20 ounces) with a handle length suited to your arm and muscle power: In other words, it should be comfortable to swing, allowing you to maintain an easy rhythm while using it. A wooden handle is traditional (and some say more comfortable), but it won't stand up as well to repeated nail pulling as a fiberglass or steel handle. I keep a number of wood-handled hammers on hand for light work, but recommend a handle of fiberglass or steel if you are contemplating heavier jobs. These materials are easier on the wrist and elbow because they absorb shock better in repetitive work.

Carpenter's handsaw (crosscut): There are two basic types of handsaw: the *crosscut saw*, designed to cut across the grain, and the *ripsaw* (with larger and fewer teeth), made to cut with the grain. The crosscut saw has a greater degree of "set"—the angle at which the teeth are positioned away from the center line of the saw. This allows the tool to cut a "kerf," or slit, larger than the body of the saw blade to prevent the blade from binding with the wood as you cut. When everything was done by hand, the two types of saw were equally important. These days, however, if you are sawing by hand at all, chances are you'll be crosscutting 99 percent of the time. Opt for an 8-point crosscut saw with a 26-inch long blade (the 8 *points*

refers to the number of teeth per inch). Handles can be wood or plastic.

Landscape (pruning) saw: This tool is for cutting small limbs and brush. The blade has two cutting edges: one with sharp crosscut teeth for deadwood and finer work and one with larger, coarser teeth for green wood.

Screwdrivers: There are more types of screwdrivers than cars. Some are highly specialized, such as the nonconductive electric screwdrivers that come complete with wire nut drivers in the handle ends. But to start your toolbox, all you really need are a couple of *Phillips* screwdrivers (no. 1 and no. 3) for cross-slot screws, and a couple of the standard *slotted* type. The slotted screwdrivers don't come in numbered sizes; just buy one in a small and one in a medium length, choosing those that feel comfortable in your hand. Wood-handled screwdrivers are getting scarce; most have handles of plastic, or plastic with a rubber coating for good gripping. As always, I like the wood, but the plastic-handled ones are more durable and come in a much larger selection.

TIP Bit by Bit Instead of shopping for individual screwdrivers, you can buy a combination set that comes with one handle and interchangeable bits designed to fit various screw heads.

Pliers: There are almost as many types and sizes of these gripping tools as there are screwdrivers. The trouble is that you can never have enough of them, and you will never be able to own one of each, so start with a few different types suited to the jobs at hand. General-purpose *pump* or *channel lock pliers*

are basically the same: They have longer handles and adjustable mouths. By contrast, square-mouth *electrician's* or *lineman's pliers*, designed to cut wires, are not adjustable. *Needle-nose pliers* are contoured to reach into small places and come in numerous shapes and sizes: Some are long and flat, others are round (for use with wire).

Retractable measuring tape: Measuring tapes come in standard lengths, from 3 to 50 feet. Tapes from 10 to 25 feet should be adequate for most jobs. I'm sorry to say that the traditional wooden folding rules are seen less and less around the working trades, although years ago everyone used them. The folding and unfolding comes automatically to me, but is slow and awkward for most people. It's faster and easier to measure longer distances with a tape. If you are in a collecting mood, though, vintage rules are still relatively inexpensive and can be quite beautiful.

Chalk line: This incredibly handy tool is used to mark straight lines between two points by snapping a chalk-covered string on a flat surface (especially good for laying out grid patterns). As the wind-up string is pulled from the refillable case, it gets coated with chalk. The chalk comes in a choice of colors: I like the traditional blue.

Pry bar (or pinch bar): This double-ended steel tool has two blades (one angled, one a curved claw). Designed for general prying and for pulling stubborn nails, the bar can also be used to get some leverage when moving heavy objects. The average length is 18 to 24 inches.

Squares: These practical flat-bladed tools are designed primarily for measuring and laying out. I recommend at least one of the three basic types: *try square, combination square,* and *framing square*. Marked in inches, the wood-handled try square is used for laying out cutting lines at 90-degree angles. It usually has an 8-inch blade. The combination square (typically 12 inches) has a sliding head, which can be adjusted to create a 90-degree square and a 45-degree miter angle. The L-shaped framing square (with 16-inch and 24-inch blades) has the most uses and is the true backbone of carpentry. It is marked with a variety of tables for figuring length of rafters and calculating angle cuts, area, and volume. It is also great for marking cuts and checking to see if things are square: With this basic tool you can learn to frame a roof or even construct a set of stairs. Squares are usually made of aluminum or steel; aluminum doesn't rust, but it can nick or bend more easily.

Spirit (or vial) level: This tool (made of wood, steel, or aluminum) contains a floating bubble designed to indicate when something is level (or not level). A two-footer should be fine for most projects. Here's a tip: When using this tool to check levels over a long distance, turn the level end over end as you go along. This will compensate for any slight discrepancy in the bubble.

Sheetrock (utility) knife: This is handy for cutting or scoring most materials; it removes slivers—and sharpens pencils, too.

Awl: The original "pencil" used to mark lines on materials, the awl is one of the oldest and most basic tool types. It resembles a short ice pick. Use it for starting screw holes and for layout work. The steel shaft is fitted with a small round wooden "ball" handle that fits naturally in the palm. Opt for one about 6 inches long.

Wood plane: There are dozens of types and even more sizes —all tailored to specific tasks that involve shaving or planing wood. I'd start with a small *block plane*; most have low-angled blades that work on a variety of wood grains, even the rough "end grains" at the end of a piece of wood. The block plane is very handy for minor projects around the house, like shaving down a door that sticks. Modern planes are made with steel blades and steel bodies; antique planes, also great collectibles, usually have wood bodies. A few rare examples are made with aluminum bodies.

Wood chisel: If you buy only one chisel, choose one with an all-purpose blade width of ½ inch or ¾ inch. Chisels are very useful, but they can be hard tools to master; they are driven by hand or mallet—but seldom by hammer. As is true of the wood plane, they should be very sharp.

Sharpening stone: Sooner rather than later you'll need to sharpen your metal-bladed tools—usually this means chisels and planes (also household knives)—which makes them easier and also safer to use. The general-purpose *Arkansas stone* is a good choice, but remember to use an oiled stone. Light (10 or 20 weight) oil is best; it prevents buildup of the metal filings and keeps the stone clean. Learning how to sharpen tools can take some time and patience, but it is incredibly rewarding. I feel no greater pride than when I am putting a new edge on one of my tools.

Power drill/screw gun: This tool features changeable bits so that you can use it for drilling or putting in screws. Opt for a model that comes with a set of high-speed twist drill bits for both metal and wood, as well as several types of screw bits. A battery-operated model is the handiest and will perform most tasks. Corded electric drills are typically used only for heavy boring and drilling.

YARD AND LANDSCAPE

■ **Make sure outdoor water systems, including pipes and faucets, are up and running.** In cold-weather regions, it is customary to drain the pipes serving potting sheds, watering systems, and pools so that they don't freeze and burst; but now everything should get turned on again. Check that your hoses and sprinklers aren't using water that is being treated with a water softener for indoor use because the sodium in softeners can be toxic to plants and grasses. Your plumber can install a separate spigot. Use unsoftened water for washing cars as well.

■ **Examine retaining walls for winter damage.** Unless your property occupies a level site, chances are good that one or more retaining walls—designed to prevent flooding and erosion on hilly land—are an integral part of your yard. Check masonry walls for cracks and frost heaves and inspect wood walls for rot, splintering, and bulges.

■ **Drain birdbaths and other receptacles,** such as planters, to get rid of water that accumulates during spring rains. This is the start of mosquito season, and nothing attracts the breeding insects quicker than a pool of stagnant water.

■ **Start preparing new garden beds.** This job should be done after the soil has completely thawed. It should be wet, but still crumbly enough to break apart easily. If you are digging a new bed in the lawn, I suggest a tool known as a sod lifter, which allows you to make a clean cut and save the grass for reuse. Use a spade or rototiller to dig the bed and aerate the soil, working in well-rotted compost or manure to add nutrients and improve drainage. The bed should be about 9 to 12 inches deep.

■ **Get existing perennial beds ready for the new season.** Clean out winter debris and remove protective boughs or other coverings. Rake out leaves and other matter that may have blown in over the last months, working gently in order not to damage the first shoots of sprouting perennials. Uncover all spring-blooming plants, carefully clip away dead and woody stems, then pull up any early weeds that you spot.

■ **Transplant and divide summer- and fall-blooming perennials.** Start when they are about three inches high. Add a couple of tablespoons of bone meal or wood ash when replanting to help them along in their new sites.

■ **Check shrubs and trees for winter damage and prune accordingly.** Remove deadwood or broken and hanging branches. Replant any shrubs that have heaved out of the soil during a freeze-thaw cycle before the roots dry out.

■ **Repair any lawn areas that have suffered winter burn and other damage** by scattering seed or laying down patches of sod. If you are using seed, cover it with a light layer of straw to help maintain moisture and protect from hungry birds.

INSIDE

- Do your fan homework.
- Clean carpets.
- Get your dehumidifier up and running.
- Put your humidifier away.
- Clean and ventilate the basement.
- Check the basement for signs of high humidity and leaks.
- Air the attic and clean it thoroughly.

OUTSIDE

- Change storm windows to screens.
- Install window-unit air conditioners.
- Put up window boxes.
- Prep exterior surfaces for painting.

DECK, PORCH, AND PATIO

- Stock up on citronella and bug repellents.
- Prepare porch and patio planters.
- Rig umbrellas and sunshades.

GARAGE AND TOOLSHED

- Set up a dehumidifier.
- Install good lighting.
- Organize your tool bench.

YARD AND LANDSCAPE

- Ready your swimming pool for use.
- Check the pool surround.
- Clean and seal blacktop.
- Clean birdbaths.
- Repair and paint trellises.
- Survey your lawn for bare spots.
- Clean winter mulch from garden beds.
- Plan new plantings.
- Fertilize your lawn.
- Plant flowers to attract birds and butterflies.
- Start fertilizing container plants.

May

Ah, the lusty month of May! No matter where you hail from, it's too late in the year for any kind of convincing procrastination. It's time to finish serious spring cleaning and to start real gardening projects. Put away the last of your winter clothes and linens, break out the summer slipcovers, and start planning for painting and repair jobs. Make a checklist and get cracking; don't wait till the day before guests are due to get your garden furniture, barbecue, and pool clean and in working order.

■ **Do your fan homework.** An *exhaust fan* (wall or ceiling) vented to the outdoors helps keep mildew at bay in a damp bathroom and expel cooking odors from a kitchen. *Ceiling fans* are great for the rest of the house, particularly in high-ceilinged rooms. These broad-bladed fans are designed to draw hot air upward. You can switch the direction in cool weather to push warm air down.

An *attic fan* (ideally set on a thermostat and usually vented to the outside) is designed to remove the hot, rising air trapped in your attic.

Located in the ceiling of an upper-level room, a *whole-house fan* vents hot air from the lower floors by sending it out through an attic space (often via a duct system that takes it outdoors). This system works best at night; the idea is to open windows so the fan can draw cool air upward. Though not a substitute for air-conditioning, a whole-house fan can still make the temperature feel substantially cooler by keeping the air moving. In moderate climates, an all-house fan may be all that's needed to maintain comfort during sticky weather.

■ **Clean carpets.** Even if you deodorized with baking soda during the winter, you should clean your carpets now that the April mud season is over. Vacuum them thoroughly, then shampoo. Supermarket cleaning products typically come as spray foam or powder, dispensed from an aerosol can. The powder dries faster, which means you can use the room sooner. The alternative is a wet-cleaning machine (or steamer), which can be rented from many supermarkets and most hardware stores. A steamer dispenses a hot shampoo solution, then sucks up the dirty residue. Some are designed to connect by hose to a hot-water faucet; others are equipped with a hot-water reservoir. Running these machines is harder work than using an aerosol spray cleaner, but it's generally much more effective.

TIP Safe Cleaning When cleaning carpets yourself, only use detergents that are made specifically for this purpose. Measure solutions precisely, according to the directions. Never clean with ordinary household soap, dishwasher detergent, laundry soap, or bleach because using such products can cause irreversible damage and may even nullify a manufacturer's warranty. Before using any cleanser, open windows and turn on ceiling fans.

TIP Going Pro Bad stains and ground-in dirt may require a professional carpet-cleaning service. Have the service make a preliminary evaluation and give you an estimate. Point out any serious stains and find out ahead of time if the service will be able to remove them without harming the carpet fibers. You should also ask how the service plans to protect your furniture—such as putting protective pads under chair and table legs.

TIP Stinging Eyes To check your sensitivity to the chemicals in new carpeting (before buying, that is), seal a sample in a glass jar and set the jar in the sunlight for 24 hours. Then open the jar and gently take a whiff—if the fumes are repellent, or irritate your eyes, make another choice.

■ **Get your dehumidifier up and running.** Although you want to moisten dry air indoors in winter, too much dampness during the spring and summer will cause problems. Unless you live in the desert Southwest, you must deal with the onset of damp, humid air almost as soon as the weather gets warm. The number-one enemy in humid climates is mildew, a common household mold that flourishes in dark, damp, poorly ventilated spaces.

The best defense against dampness is a dehumidifier. These handy machines work by blowing air over open refrigeration coils; as the air passes over the coils, moisture from the air condenses and drips into a collection tray or pail. A simple portable model will serve most household needs. It should go where the moisture is—in a damp basement or any room that is partially or completely underground.

To prevent overflowing, most dehumidifiers are equipped with a float mechanism that turns the machine off automatically when the water it has collected reaches a certain level. The collection pail may need to be emptied up to two or three times a day—which means it's convenient to locate the dehumidifier somewhere reasonably near a sink. Standing water also breeds bacteria—another reason to empty it often. To avoid the dumping process, you can have a dehumidifier empty directly into a sewer line or basement drain.

■ **Put your humidifier away.** Clean it thoroughly and make sure it is dry before you store it. Throw away any demineralization cartridges, cassettes, and filters and store everything in a clean, dry place.

■ **Clean and ventilate the basement.** Even if you cleaned up last autumn, dirt and cobwebs will have accumulated over the winter. Open doors and windows and give your cellar or basement a spring airing. Sweep it thoroughly or vacuum with a shop vacuum. Cleaning helps keep out mildew and insects, which thrive in dust and clogged areas. Check nooks and crannies for rodent nests.

■ **Check the basement for signs of high humidity and leaks.** Cold-water pipes are a likely trouble spot for water condensation. Dry any wet cold-water pipes thoroughly with a cloth, then cover them with foam insulators. This will prevent condensation that comes from the contact of warm, moist air with the pipes. (The insulation will also help protect the pipes from the freezing temperatures of winter.)

■ **Air the attic and clean it thoroughly.** Check for insect or rodent infestation and leaks from water that may have seeped inside from under the chimney.

TIP Making Spring Flowers Last Cut tulips early in the morning, *before* buds start to open. Place the stems up to their necks in lukewarm water and set them in a cool location for 12 hours before arranging them. This strategy also extends the life of peonies by a good margin.

CARING FOR RUGS

The old spring-cleaning ritual of hanging throw rugs on a clothesline and beating out the winter's dirt was designed to rid carpets of the grime and soot produced by gas and oil lamps; rug beaters were commonly used until the early 1900s, when the electric vacuum began to supplant them. Today, vacuuming remains the recommended method for light rug cleaning. Vintage and antique rugs, in particular, should never be beaten or shaken, because this damages the backing and fibers. If a throw rug needs washing and can withstand it, test for colorfastness by wetting a small, inconspicuous area with cold water, and blotting with a clean white cloth. If the colors do not bleed, you should be able to wash the rug safely using a sponge. Dip the sponge in a solution of cold water and mild fabric detergent, then squeeze it almost dry. Rub the rug surface gently in a circular motion with the detergent solution, then rinse by rubbing cold water using the same motion.

Avoid exposing an antique rug to excessive wear or direct sunlight. To protect the backing, use a synthetic-fiber underlay. Never fold or put an old rug in a plastic bag to store it. Lay it flat or roll it loosely, front side out, and protect it with a clean sheet or towel.

And those rug beaters? Save them for display. More than 150 types of rug beater were made in America alone, and these sculptural objects are still readily available at flea markets and antique shops.

VINTAGE FANS

In the days before air-conditioning, the best defense against the heat of the day was the once-common window awning. The first commercially manufactured electric fan was introduced in 1882 by the American firm of Crocker and Curtis. During the early 20th century, these appliances were considered a luxury because high prices put them beyond the reach of most homeowners. By the 1920s, however, advances in steel technology and mass production made electric fans more affordable. When their makers began competing for sales with innovations ranging from oscillating necks to specially contoured Bakelite blades, the fan came into its own as an object of industrial design. Some of the most notable examples now popular among collectors are the streamlined Art Deco designs of the late 1920s and early 1930s. Check your attic: Vintage fans can bring prices upward of $500.

OUTSIDE

■ **Change storm windows to screens.** If screens are really dirty, clean them before you install them by vacuuming the surface with a brush attachment. Then rinse with a hose.

■ **Install window-unit air conditioners.** Go over the unit with the brush attachment of your vacuum. Remove the filter, wash it under a running faucet, then dry and reinstall it.

■ **Put up window boxes.** Dump the previous season's dirt and clean out boxes thoroughly. Fit wooden boxes with waterproof liners or plastic garbage bags to protect the wood from moisture and keep paint from peeling. Make sure there are drainage holes. Replant the boxes using sterile potting soil after you're sure the last frost date has passed.

■ **Prep exterior surfaces for painting by scraping and priming properly.** Prep work is time consuming but critical to the success of a paint job. If you take the time to do it and do it well, you won't find yourself with a rush job when warm weather sets in. A good exterior paint job on properly prepared surfaces (see "Tips on House Painting," June) should last for an average of seven years, although a few touch-ups might be needed. If the top layer of paint has broken down into a powdery chalk, new paint will not adhere to the surface; you'll need to wash the area with a detergent or bleach solution and rinse. Let the surface dry for two or three days before repainting.

CHECKING TAX ASSESSMENTS

Did you know that you have a legal right to challenge the tax assessment on your home? In my region, revised tax assessments go on file at the assessor's office in the spring; check your own office for its calendar. Homeowners are notified of a change in assessment or a change in rates by mail. The frequency of reevaluation varies from town to town; properties might be reevaluated every 5 years or as seldom as every 25. Some states require such a "reval" at specific intervals. The number of years depends on many variables: a town's need to raise cash, pressure to equalize rates in the same county, a rise in complaints.

If you think an evaluation is unfair and want to challenge it, you must do your own research. Start by contacting the town clerk or assessor and checking the property taxes in your area, which are a matter of town record. Seeing how your neighbors have been assessed helps you make a comparison. Tax officials may have assessed your property for amenities and improvements that don't exist. You can also raise questions prompted by comparisons: Why is a new house of comparable size in the same neighborhood assessed lower than your older house? You may find that your property qualifies for an exclusion or abatement.

Look for notes from the assessment explaining how it was determined and find out what the state guidelines are. Houses and improvements are classified as type A, B, and C construction, which refers to quality levels and the value of construction. The lack or inclusion of basements, attics, crawl spaces, and outbuildings and the size and amenities of the property are all calculated. Be sure that you are comparing the value of a property that is reasonably equivalent to yours and ask about the deadline for filing a grievance. If the ruling goes against you, it's possible to file a legal appeal. When deciding whether an appeal is worth the cost and effort, consider the amount of assessment, the tax base, and the projected period of ownership.

DECK, PORCH, AND Patio

■ **Stock up on citronella and bug repellents.** Use all repellents, especially those that burn with wicks, carefully. If mosquitoes are a serious problem, you may want to try one of the new silent mosquito traps, which work by attracting bugs with a combination of heat and carbon dioxide. Although expensive, they can be very effective.

■ **Prepare porch and patio planters.** Like window boxes, these should be completely clean. Built-in planters should be fitted with waterproof liners and made from a moisture-resistant natural material, such as redwood, cedar, cypress, or pressure-treated wood. Annuals and perennials require a depth of about 10 to 14 inches; planters for shrubs

and miniature trees should be 18 to 24 inches deep. Make sure all freestanding planters rest on a protective saucer to catch runoff from watering because water draining through a flowerpot will quickly rot wood flooring and stain virtually any surface. Built-in planters need to drain (via holes in the bottom) directly through the decking or porch floor to the ground underneath.

TIP Green Grout If your patio is paved with irregularly shaped flagstones set in sand or another "dry mortar," such as stone dust, you're already aware that this material can wash out easily in a heavy rain. When laying down a new surface, consider planting the gaps between stones with a natural ground cover like candytuft, alyssum, moss, or any variety of flowering thyme.

■ **Rig umbrellas and sunshades**. Make sure umbrellas are properly secured in weighted stands. With the umbrella secure, open it and clean it by vacuuming with a brush attachment or by damp-wiping.

TIP Only Your Gardener Knows for Sure Going natural may be fashionable these days, but anybody who has tried to move a large clay pot or planter after it's filled with wet potting soil may want to yield to practicality. Consider a planter made of a synthetic material; these are lightweight, durable, and less prone to cracking and damage than clay pots. Some are so well designed that even in a close-up inspection it's hard to tell that they are not real pottery.

HOME *Almanac*

GARAGE
AND
*T*OOLSHED

■ **Set up a dehumidifier.** If you have a basement or garage workshop, chances are it's damp. Dry air helps keep tools from rusting, and keeping humidity levels even helps to prevent lumber from warping. A dry environment is also preferable for using glues, paints, and varnishes. They'll cure faster, and fumes won't linger in the air as long. All in all, you'll have a healthier climate for puttering.

■ **Install good lighting.** For safety, you need good light for using tools and reading the labels on paints, insect sprays, and varnishes. Protect bulbs in your workspace with a lens or safety screen to avoid accidental smashes. An unprotected bulb can get broken easily when you're carrying a ladder, for example, or moving lumber around.

■ **Organize your tool bench and get rid of the detritus.** Have work and garden gloves handy and keep a first-aid kit, including eyewash, on hand for an emergency.

YARD
AND
ᴌANDSCAPE

■ **Ready your swimming pool for use.** Check to see whether cleaning equipment like nylon brushes and skimmers is in good shape. Stock up on chemicals and be sure your water-testing kit is complete. If you lowered the water level in the fall, you need to fill the pool now. If all this is beyond you, hire a pool-cleaning service. Spend some time with the professional who services your pool so you can learn the process yourself.

■ **Check the pool surround to make sure that decking and pavers are in good shape after winter wear and tear.** Inspect wood for warping and splinters, slate for heaving, and

concrete for cracks. Make repairs as needed to prevent accidents.

- **Clean and seal blacktop.** If you have a blacktop driveway, you should do this at least once a year. Use a high-quality commercial cleanser to remove grease and oil first; next, a good going-over with a pressure washer will help rinse away dirt and weeds. Clean out any cracks and repair them with driveway filler, then follow with a good commercial sealer. Concrete drives and walks should also be cleaned and sealed with products made for this purpose. The staff at a good hardware store can advise you about purchasing supplies and equipment—or you can turn the job over to a pro.

- **Clean birdbaths**, using a mild, nontoxic soap solution and a wire brush to remove scum. Rinse the basin thoroughly after cleaning and fill it with fresh water. Change the water regularly.

- **Repair and paint trellises.** Do this now, before vines and climbing plants have a chance to grow.

- **Survey your lawn for bare spots.** Brown patches should be cleared of dead grass and reseeded. Break up the top few inches of soil with a claw and reseed with a variety suitable for your climate and region and for sun or shade, then lightly fertilize. The traditional method for keeping the seeds from being eaten by birds or blown away in the wind is to cover the newly planted areas with straw. A good alternative is a layer of peat moss or Penn Mulch, a paper-based product. Either will keep the seeds moist and protected. Water well and cut the grass when it gets to be about three inches tall to promote root development.

- **Clean winter mulch from garden beds.** If you have added evergreens or any other mulches during the fall and winter to prevent perennials

from heaving, remove them before the first spell of warm weather. Otherwise the old mulch will continue to act as a protective cover, smothering new growth by screening out the light and air that your garden beds desperately need at this time of year.

After perennials have started sprouting, gently rake the beds and add a layer of fresh mulch or compost. These supply nutrients to the soil as they decompose and help keep weeds at bay. Replenish them as needed to maintain a light covering of two to three inches. Leave the bases of plants free of the protective covering to allow air circulation and prevent rotting.

■ **Plan new plantings.** Begin planting annuals and adding perennials after the last frost date. Needless to say, shopping for plants is tempting at this time of year. If you see something you want at your garden center early in the month, buy it, because stocks can get depleted early. More than once I've returned later in the season to get something when I'm ready to plant only to find that it's sold out. If it's too early to plant, shelter the flats and temporary pots indoors at night while you wait for milder weather.

■ **Fertilize your lawn.** A high-nitrogen fertilizer should be applied twice a year, once in spring and once in fall. If a weed killer is needed, use an organic one, or try to be accepting of a less-than-perfect lawn!

■ **Plant flowers to attract birds and butterflies.** Birds feast on insect pests such as mosquitoes and their eggs and larvae, and butterflies are valuable pollinators. Both are a delight to watch. Asters, bachelor's

HOME *A*LMANAC

buttons, black-eyed Susans, coreopsis, phlox, poppies, and marigolds all produce seeds that entice birds; hummingbirds are particularly attracted to the nectar of red and orange flowers, such as trumpet vine blossoms. Bee balm, blanketflowers, asters, astilbe, cosmos, heliotrope, Shasta daisies, yarrow, and zinnias are among the annuals and perennials that lure butterflies.

■ **Start fertilizing container plants.** Most potted garden plants—annuals, perennials, shrubs, and even small trees—need more attention than plants growing in the ground. That means frequent watering and regular feedings. For annuals, use a liquid fertilizer once a week. Start perennials off with a time-released fertilizer that stays in the pot and releases food to the plant with each watering. To spurt immediate growth, supplement with an organic fertilizer. Potted roses should also be fed once a month with rose food for continual bloom. Containers should be large enough to accommodate root growth—at least an inch wider than the root ball. If there are no drainage holes, place an inch-deep layer of gravel in the base of the container before adding the potting soil mixture. A good all-purpose recipe is one part perlite, one part peat moss or compost, and two parts good, sterile potting soil.

TIP Never Mow a Wet Lawn
This is hard on your mower and also hard on the grass, which will just go flat under the blades. The result is a ragged, unhealthy cut.

THINGS TO DO IN JUNE

INSIDE

- Let in fresh air.
- Launch an attack on indoor pests.
- Make sure all faucets and pipes are dry.
- Change your furnace filter.

OUTSIDE

- Clean gutters.
- Wash your home's siding.
- Check caulking.

DECK, PORCH, AND PATIO

- Water and fertilize planters often.
- Clean outdoor furniture regularly.
- Rearrange outdoor furniture to take advantage of changing sun and shade patterns.
- Consider a privacy screen.

GARAGE AND TOOLSHED

- Keep tools and equipment oiled and sharpened.
- Read owner's manuals for maintenance tips.
- Check your safety gear.

YARD AND LANDSCAPE

- Maintain the swimming pool.
- Experiment with movable containers.
- Continue adding annuals and perennials to garden beds.
- Weed regularly.
- Deadhead late spring–flowering shrubs.
- Plant vegetable seeds and add varieties for fall harvests.
- Mow grass once a week or every 10 days to encourage healthy growth.

June

*M*other *Nature* would have trouble producing a more beautiful—or fickle—month. June is a true temptress: Just when those clear days convince you that you'll never have to turn on an air conditioner, the haze and humidity set in (not to mention the bugs). And just when your flower beds look perfect (I still think the best perennials bloom this month), a storm blows all the blossoms off the peonies and a drought sets in (not to mention the bugs). My advice? Enjoy June, no matter how unpredictable it is. Before long you'll be wishing for the return of early summer.

INSIDE

■ **Let in fresh air.** On dry days, throw open windows and doors. When the air is cooler outside than inside, open your attic windows to let the rising hot air out, and open downstairs windows to bring cool air in. If you have allergies or respiratory problems, consider having an air cleaner or filter installed in your heating-duct system. Air filters can also be integrated directly into air-conditioning ductwork. The alternative is a portable room air filter. I recommend the electronic type, which is the most efficient and easiest to clean.

■ **Launch an attack on indoor pests.** I can always tell that it's June when the annual parade of black ants starts making its way into the house. This is also the season for flies, mealworms, grain moths, roaches, fleas, and other bugs that hatch or thrive in warm weather. Bugs and rodents are looking for nourishment, so the logical approach is to limit their food and water sources. Store dry goods like flour, grains, chocolate, dry soup, cereal, and sugar in tightly sealed containers. Fit whatever you can in the refrigerator, because cold kills bugs, or at least slows them down. Wash dog and cat dishes immediately after your pet has finished eating and put garbage in a tightly sealed can or bag. Clean all containers being saved for recycling. Check for gaps around telephone and electrical wires, outlets and TV cables, ducts and heating pipes. Stuff these small entry points with steel wool (mice hate it) or wire mesh and caulk to cover openings.

■ **Make sure all faucets and pipes are dry.** Condensation and standing water are insect magnets. Check for leaks around bathroom, laundry, and kitchen fixtures. Wet wood is a nesting site for carpenter ants, and nurtures mold, mildew, and dry rot.

■ **Change your furnace filter.** Most central air-conditioning systems are combination systems that share furnace ducts. In this case, central air conditioning puts extra pressure on your furnace system because the fan has to work harder to process cool air, which is heavier than warm air. Change the filter, or at least clean it, twice a year.

TIP Natural Insect Repellents Marauding pests tend to target the kitchen, which is one place where I never want to use a chemical insecticide. To repel ants, wipe down countertops with vinegar or a solution of citrus oil and water. Among other natural insect repellents are bay leaves, which discourage roaches (they also hate garlic), and mealworms. Try tucking a few bay leaves into packages of flour and other dry foods. Another traditional method for keeping ants away is to sprinkle crushed dried mint leaves or black pepper in the bottom of your trash can. Basil and tansy are good insect repellents as well.

To kill or deter bugs, try zapping them with a solution of 1 tablespoon liquid dish detergent to 1 quart water. Spritzing with soap kills ants on contact and helps eliminate the scent trails they leave for other members of their colony. A few saucers of the soapy liquid set strategically around the kitchen will also serve as natural ant traps.

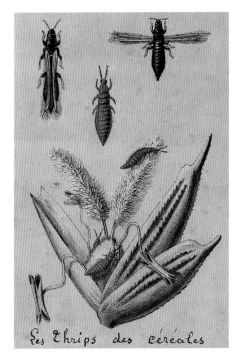

Les Thrips des céréales

VINTAGE TINS

An enduring form of advertising art, tin-plated boxes and bins decorated with slogans and enticing images of the goods packaged inside were introduced in the mid-1800s, initially by British and French biscuit manufacturers. Although tin-plated containers were used for packaging much earlier, not until this period was the technology available for printing directly on the containers. This innovation eliminated the need to supply separate or printed labels, and also proved a brilliant advertising strategy; people couldn't resist saving the tins after they had used up the contents. The cocoa, tobacco, tea, coffee, marshmallows, spices, or mustard might be gone, but the advertisement for that product endured in the colorful wording and images. Vintage tins can still be used—to store foods and to keep bugs out. To protect vintage tins from rusting and fading, keep them away from moisture and direct sunlight. To clean an undecorated interior of rust and grime, rub gently with fine steel wool. Clean the exteriors with a nonabrasive liquid metal polish or mild soap and a soft cloth. Dry them well.

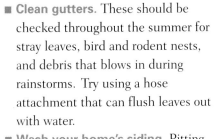

OUTSIDE

■ **Clean gutters.** These should be checked throughout the summer for stray leaves, bird and rodent nests, and debris that blows in during rainstorms. Try using a hose attachment that can flush leaves out with water.

■ **Wash your home's siding.** Pitting from dirt is a problem for vinyl and aluminum siding, which cannot be painted when they start to look dingy. Keeping siding clean is the best line of attack against deterioration, and the easiest way is to use a pressure washer. Now is also a good time to check wood

siding and shingles for water damage. If you see rusty nails, there's a good chance that the siding is consistently wet—possibly because rain water is draining down behind clapboards or shingles. If you think this is the case, have a professional check it out. Always keep plantings cut back so that air can circulate and allow the siding to dry. And clean those gutters!

■ **Check caulking.** Inspect the areas around trim, vents, spigots, and entry points for wiring by pressing with a screwdriver. Good caulking feels pliant and springs back; bad caulking (caulking that has dried out) is hard and brittle to the touch. In this case, the old caulking should be stripped out and replaced with new. Always choose high-quality caulk: Cheap material does not install as well, last as long, or remain pliable throughout its life. Different applications require different types of caulk. Pure silicone or a strong silicone blend is effective for metal (especially copper and aluminum) and glass. A good exterior latex or acrylic caulk with some silicone for longevity and workability is best for painted or stained wood and for use around doors and windows. Check the labels of the numerous types available for content and application.

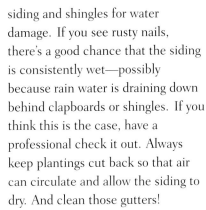

TIPS ON HOUSE PAINTING

The rule of thumb for exterior painting is not to schedule it when the temperature may fall below 40°F, because the surfaces must remain dry and fairly warm. Freezing conditions cause the water in latex paint to separate and prevent alkyd paint from drying, so that it won't soak in or adhere to the surface properly. The longer paint remains tacky, the more dirt, bugs, and leaves get stuck in it.

Good preparation is the key to all painting success. The concept is simple if you picture the paint going onto the surface: Anything the paint is touching, like a layer of grit, is going to show. The more easily the paint can soak in and dry properly, the longer-lasting and better-looking the job will be. Loose paint must be scraped off, and raw wood or metal should be sanded and free of dirt and dust. Filling nail holes and caulking cracks is important because these tasks prevent moisture from getting under the paint. Letting moisture infiltrate is the surest way to shorten the life of a paint job; it encourages peeling, blistering, and possibly rot.

Painters

Good painters are worth their weight in gold. Check out painting contractors the same way you would investigate any other tradesperson or contractor. In particular, look for a painter who is neat and clean. If a painter greets me looking as though he or she is the paintbrush, I wonder if the work will look the same—sloppy and unprofessional. I have found that a good painter comes to the job looking like any other tradesperson. He or she changes into painter's overalls, works in a neat and orderly manner all day, then cleans up the space, tools, and him- or herself before leaving the job.

Painting is the easiest building trade to get into because it requires only minimal training and a small investment in supplies and equipment. So be sure to check on a prospective painter's experience and references.

Colors that invite repose

IN the bedroom, whether the furnishings are simple or sumptuous, good taste demands a background in complete concordance. Walls tinted with Nature's Harmony of soft colors merge into a pleasing composite that appeals to the eye and invites repose.

KEYSTONA is a flat linseed oil paint which comes in a variety of shades from the most delicate of tapestry tints to the rich, full hues of velvet hangings. Easily applied and dries with a smooth, dull surface resembling wall paper.

There is a KEYSTONE Finish for every interior purpose, in a wide variety of colors.

Booklets and color charts are sent gladly upon request.

KEYSTONA may be washed repeatedly with soap and water — the colors remaining bright and the walls sanitary.

KEYSTONE VARNISH COMPANY
Hull, England   Brooklyn, N.Y.

KEYSTONA
FLAT FINISH

Don't skimp on painting standards. The plaster, drywall, and carpentry might be of the highest quality, but if the painting is done poorly, nothing will look as it should. A good painter will find and correct small blemishes and actually improve the quality of the overall project.

Calculating Paint Needs

One gallon of paint usually covers about 350 square feet (400 tops). To calculate the amount of paint (or primer) needed for one coat, measure the roof height and the perimeter and multiply the two figures, then divide by 350. Check the label of the paint products you choose for information on coverage under special conditions.

The rougher the surface (shingles, for instance), the more paint you will need: Reduce the estimate to about one gallon per 250 or 300 square feet. For every six gallons of house paint, count on one gallon for the trim.

UNDERSTANDING SEPTIC SYSTEMS

You may not have considered that the water from showers, washing machines, and all the plumbing equipment in your home needs a place to go when you rinse, flush, or run the dishwasher. There are two basic types of waste disposal systems: One is a municipal sewer system that accommodates many households in a given area and processes the waste off-site; the other is a septic system, essentially a mini-sewer system designed to process your home's waste on your property.

If there are no sidewalks in front of your home, you probably have a septic system. The systems generally consist of a main line running from the house into an underground tank outside, where solids sink to the bottom and are processed into liquid that flows into a leaching field. This contains a series of pipes buried in gravel to allow the water effluent to seep gradually and safely into the ground. If the system is working properly, the tank needs pumping only occasionally—about every three to five years, depending on the number of people using the system.

Some old houses have a cesspool (a tank or pool) only. Instead of draining into a leaching field, liquid leaches directly into the soil surrounding the tank or pool. These outdated systems are not particularly efficient and tend to fail frequently, especially if the demand on them suddenly increases—as when a new homeowner moves in with five kids. Cesspool systems should be replaced; in many areas of the country they are now illegal. When you buy a home, make sure you have its system checked during the house inspection. That process tells you what you have, where it is, and whether it is working properly.

"Standard"
PLUMBING FIXTURES

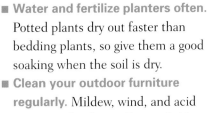

DECK,

PORCH,

AND

*P*ATIO

■ **Water and fertilize planters often.** Potted plants dry out faster than bedding plants, so give them a good soaking when the soil is dry.

■ **Clean your outdoor furniture regularly.** Mildew, wind, and acid rain can take their toll remarkably fast once summer gets going. A nonabrasive all-purpose spray cleaner and soft cloth work well for most furniture types.

■ **Rearrange outdoor furniture to take advantage of changing sun and shade patterns.** No law says that furniture has to stay where you placed it when you first put it out in the spring. Arrange your furniture to take advantage of more direct sun in the cool mornings, and position your favorite chaise or hammock to catch the shade during the hottest part of the day.

■ **Consider a privacy screen.** A trellis or screen of latticework or slatted boards can provide a buffer for a driveway or close neighbor while letting air circulate. You can plant climbing vines to provide texture and create a natural look.

TIP Plants on the Run

To make moving large planters around easier, set them on a base or platform fitted with casters. Most garden centers offer planters already equipped with wheels.

WICKER

The name *wicker* is actually a catchall term for furniture and other goods made from a variety of materials, including woven rattan, willow, rush, reed, cane, grasses, and other natural fibers that stand up to the elements reasonably well and "breathe" easily in hot weather. Wicker first gained broad popularity in America in the mid-1800s; the furniture was believed to be good for one's health because the loose weave allowed air to circulate and made the pieces relatively easy to clean—distinct hygienic advantages over heavy upholstery.

The roots of the Victorian American wicker industry date to 1844, when a grocer named Cyrus Wakefield began experimenting with wicker packing material from the Orient found discarded on the Boston wharves. In 1855 he opened the Wakefield Rattan Company in South Reading, Massachusetts, by introducing an early line of water-resistant cane furniture for garden and lawn. The subsequent use of the reed, which is more pliant, made possible the elaborate designs so closely associated with Victorian wicker design.

One well-known successor to Cyrus Wakefield was Marshall Lloyd, a manufacturer of wicker baby carriages who invented a special loom for weaving wicker from paper fiber. By the 1920s most American wicker was made by the Lloyd loom process, which produced furniture in more closely woven, boxy designs than the ornate Victorian prototypes of the mid- to late-1800s. The use of cushions evolved during the Lloyd loom era, primarily because the machine-made furniture lacked the comfortable flexibility of the earlier wicker made by Wakefield and his competitors.

Wicker has good lasting power. Great buys still appear at auctions and tag sales, and the furniture can be easily rejuvenated with paint. The most common problems include loose leg wrappings, broken spokes, and splintered weaving, and all are relatively easy to fix on your own. Replacement materials (new wrapping pieces, spokes, and weavers) are widely available at craft shops. It is best to add the new materials by wrapping and threading so that they are held in place naturally by tension. Nails can rust, and glue will usually crack over time as the natural fibers expand and contract. To clean wicker, vacuum with a brush attachment and wash with a mild, sudsy soap solution. Rinse and dry it thoroughly.

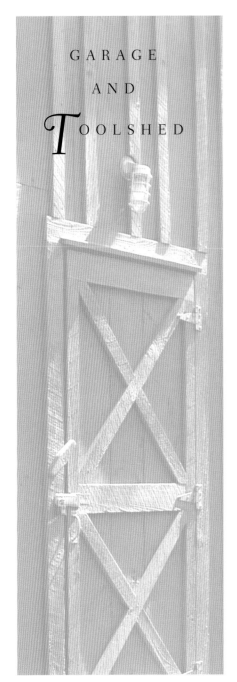

GARAGE
AND
*T*OOLSHED

■ **Keep tools and equipment oiled and sharpened.** A light coating with a good oil, such as 3-in-One or WD-40, prevents rust and corrosion on tools. Dull tools or those not in tip-top shape are dangerous—a hazard that is frequently overlooked for the sake of convenience. Just one cut with a dull blade, however, can make the blade slip because you're forced to apply too much pressure. Unsharpened blades on electric tools can also cause the tool to overheat and the motor to blow. Maintaining good tools in excellent condition can really help prevent most accidents.

■ **Read owner's manuals for maintenance tips.** Because you are about to give lawn and landscape equipment a workout, be sure you know the proper maintenance routines.

■ **Check your safety gear.** Invest in the proper items to go with the tools you use—goggles, gloves, ear mufflers, and good work boots.

MANUFACTURED BY

■ **Maintain the swimming pool.**
By keeping your pool and the surrounding areas in excellent shape, you will save money in the long run with fewer repair bills. Well-tuned equipment means more energy efficiency and lower fuel bills as well. Always follow the instructions and guidelines provided by your installer or pool-maintenance service. Heaters should be monitored and adjusted according to the temperature outside. They should be cleaned, and filters and pumps serviced as recommended; skimmers and

automatic pool cleaners also need regular care.

- **Experiment with movable containers to add spots of color and fragrance to your yard.** It's okay to continue to plant containers throughout the first part of the summer. If you space out your planting, you can see how your original combinations of plants are working, then repeat the successes or adjust as necessary.

Because movable containers permit you to create a microclimate that is especially well suited to a particular plant, you can also try growing things in pots that you wouldn't consider for your beds. A tender shade-loving plant like a fern, for example, might get parched in a sunny garden bed, but will thrive when potted in properly prepared soil, and hung in a cool spot under a tree.

Using lightweight containers, like an old tin bucket or a slatted wine crate (rather than a heavy stone or concrete urn), makes moving potted plants into sun and shade as needed much easier. You can also reposition the plants around your garden beds to add spots of color in bare patches or in areas where your perennials have already faded.

- **Continue adding annuals and perennials to garden beds.** Water all new plantings deeply by soaking them with a hose. With the water running slowly (not too strong a flow, or the water will dig a trough), set your garden hose next to plants for 10 to 15 minutes, before moving it to another spot. You might try

soaker hoses or consider installing an underground watering system on timers. Water will then be more efficiently released in small amounts directly to the soil in beds. Water plants in the morning so that the sun can dry wet leaves later in the day to prevent fungus and mildew from growing.

- **Weed regularly.** As you water, you'll be feeding seeds and plants you *don't* want. Weeds and lawn grass will migrate quickly into garden beds and compete for nutrients. They also look terrible, so you should weed often, or at least once a week.
- **Deadhead late spring–flowering shrubs**. Azaleas, rhododendrons, laurels, and lilacs need to have dead blossoms snipped off soon after flowering. You can increase the flower power of lilacs for the next year by clipping the old heads at the base within three weeks after the blooms die.
- **Plant vegetable seeds and add varieties for fall harvests**. Rutabagas, beets, collards, winter squash, pumpkins, and melons will all extend the life of your vegetable garden well into the fall.
- **Mow grass once a week or every 10 days to encourage healthy growth.** In dry weather mow less to let taller grass shade itself. To protect tree trunks from mower blades, consider creating simple garden beds around tree bases; there is still plenty of time to plant myrtle and pachysandra. Adding beds of easy-care foliage plants is a relatively simple way to give your lawn a neat, landscaped look.

Nº 28.

CERVUS VIRGINIANUS, PENNANT.
COMMON OR VIRGINIAN DEER.

Drawn from Nature by J.W. Audubon.

A hundred years ago white-tailed deer, nearly eradicated by unregulated hunting, had virtually disappeared from much of the East. As early as 1661, a deer reserve was established to stem the decline in Maryland, where some naturalists thought the animals were locally extinct. By the end of the next century, the deer had vanished from large areas of the Atlantic seaboard, and the trend continued throughout the 1800s as encroaching civilization began to limit ranging areas.

Well, they're back. One consequence of the regeneration of Eastern forests during recent decades is the recovery of these and numerous other woodland species, especially wild turkeys. The turkeys don't seem to do much in my yard besides stomping around noisily and looking clownish, but deer can be a real problem. They're beautiful, but they're also hungry, and increasingly undisturbed by human activity. If the deer are hungry enough, almost nothing will stop them from trying to get food (often in the form of your bulbs, vegetables, flowers, and ornamental shrubs). Because they're smart and adapt easily, try to vary your battle tactics often. Otherwise, the deer will catch on fast. Short of an eight-foot-high fence, consider the following strategies:

■ **Strong aromas.** The urine of deer predators, such as bears and wolves, is a natural deterrent. Special "urine kits" designed for garden and yard are widely available. Other ideas for natural solutions include garlic bulbs, small tallow-based soap bars, and fabric softener sheets (best suspended in a cheesecloth pouch). Some people drill a little hole in the soap bars and hang them from shrubs. Garlic bulbs can be "planted" around the edge of garden beds. If all else fails, try a commercial deer spray, but alternate brands often.

■ **Unappetizing flavors.** Try this recipe: Mix 3 eggs with 2 tablespoons cayenne pepper in a gallon of water. Use a mister to spray the solution on plants. Deer are repelled by sharp, spicy flavors, and as herbivores, they won't like the eggs, either.

■ **"Deer Resistant" Plants.** If you can't keep deer out of your garden, here are some flowers and shrubs they don't like:

Allium	Daisy	Barberry
Artemesia	Foxglove	Butterfly bush
Columbine	Tansy	Spirea

SUMMER

Because rain was scarce this spring, the hay harvest is starting late. Looking down the valley from our back porch, I can see my neighbor on his tractor, making the first cut in the large open field at the north end of my road. Having known this farmer for 30 years, I have the greatest respect for men like him who work every day of their lives, tilling the land and caring for the animals entrusted to them. The first night of his life was spent on this farm, in the kitchen where he was born, and Dick, now 75 years old, has never slept anywhere else. Even when he was found in the field with his arm badly injured, he refused to stay overnight in the hospital. Only he knew the milking schedule—and which cows needed special attention.

The way we live today—running about and hurrying away every other weekend—makes my neighbor's story sound like another time and place. Yet to remember this other side of life gives us great perspective. Dick is happy and fulfilled; the contentment in his voice comes from a lifetime of caring for his homestead. Like his father and grandfather, he has worked this farm every day.

Most of us don't need to work as hard as Dick or our predecessors. Our homes are also much easier to maintain. The springhouse, the corn crib, the wagon house, the summer kitchen, the root cellar, and many other farm outbuildings are now obsolete. Yet their functions are still here, contained within the walls of the modern house. The springhouse is now the refrigerator; the corn crib and root cellar are the pantry; the wagon house is the garage. Unless you are fortunate enough to own a farm with all its outbuildings intact, chances are you have to maintain only one, or maybe two, structures on your property. And many of us consider that enough.

Like my grandfather, my neighbor has a garden for vegetables, herbs, and flowers. I can remember as a young boy seeing my grandfather—who at age 75 still put in a full day's work—relaxing in the evening by gardening for two or three hours. Dick enjoys his garden in the same way. So use these months to involve yourself in a garden—get your hands in the dirt, nurture the plants, and anticipate the coming harvest—one of the great rewards in life. This is also a good time to putter around the house. Above all, savor the season. The pleasures of summer are all too fleeting.

INSIDE

- Nurture your houseplants.
- Ventilate often.
- Spot-check for mildew.
- Keep your dehumidifier(s) running.
- Regularly clean all areas prone to dampness.
- Allergy-proof your vacuum.

OUTSIDE

- Inspect walls and roof for mildew and moss.
- Maintain gutters and leaders.
- Be prepared for hurricanes and other storms.
- Run a safety check after every summer storm.

DECK, PORCH, AND PATIO

- Keep built-in planters and window boxes watered and fertilized.
- Cool down paving surfaces.
- Use plants to make a natural sun screen.
- Limit use of porch lights.

GARAGE AND TOOLSHED

- Storm-proof garage doors.
- Ventilate work spaces frequently.
- Install a tire bumper.

YARD AND LANDSCAPE

- Don't give up on weeding.
- If you didn't mulch earlier, do it now.
- Water, water, water.
- Deadhead annuals and perennials.
- Fill in with annuals.
- Stake tall plants.
- Prune maples, birches, lindens, and horse chestnuts.

July

As the summer unfolds, projects outside will take up more and more time. The logical reason is that you use your garden, deck, and porch more at this time of year, and quite simply, the weather in most parts of the country permits you to get more done outside. But don't neglect the inside of your house. Air-conditioning systems can get overworked, so keep the filters clean and use fans whenever you can to save energy.

INSIDE

■ **Nurture your houseplants.** The summer season is the danger zone for houseplants: We all tend to neglect plants inside while we focus on our gardens. To keep leafy plants free of dust, put them in the sink and spritz or treat them to a light watering and cleaning by placing them under a gentle stream of cool water in your shower stall. Deadhead and pinch off old stems to encourage bushier regrowth. Keep plants watered when you go away on vacation by using capillary watering trays (available at plant stores) designed to keep the bottoms of pots wet. Never let water collect in the saucers underneath pots, or they will become watering holes for bugs in warm weather.

■ **Ventilate often.** Keeping spaces closed up in hot weather effectively chokes off the air supply that allows your house to "breathe" the way it should at this time of year. In a very damp basement, using a portable fan is an effective way to supplement your dehumidifier. Aiming a fan or two into corners to stir up the air in these "dead" areas helps the dehumidifier do its job better by keeping the air moving and increasing the absorption of water from damp surfaces into the air. During a heat wave, keep your attic windows open day and night to create an escape hatch for hot air (which rises). An unventilated attic will collect hot air and become a stifling blanket of heat for the entire house. Venting a crawl space temporarily can be as simple as opening the access door or using a fan. A more permanent solution is to install vents to the outside to create some natural cross ventilation. You can also purchase a permanent exhaust fan to pull moist air to the outside.

Airing the basement, which helps draw cool air in, is another way to battle mildew. Keep basement doors and windows open when you are home. If you must close the house up when leaving for vacation, a weekend, or a work week in the city, air it thoroughly the day before departing and as soon as you return.

- **Spot-check your basement, bathrooms, and closets for mildew.** Keep your bathroom aired by running the fan and opening windows. Mildew (usually a whitish or greenish coating of spotty film) thrives in any dark, poorly ventilated space, making your home a breeding ground for allergies. You can control the spread of mildew in small enclosed areas like closets by occasionally leaving a light on to raise the temperature and lower the relative humidity. (Be sure that no stored items, like hats piled on a top shelf, can come in contact with the bulb.) When you spy mildew, wash down the walls and floors with a mold fungicide or liquid chlorine bleach, following the manufacturer's directions. Spot test the area first and rinse and dry thoroughly.

- **Keep your dehumidifier(s) running.** In most parts of the country that are prone to humidity, July is a month of long, hot, moist days. Mildew thrives in damp air and can be a real health threat, causing allergies and respiratory problems. Wash the dehumidifier basin out and dry off the coils to keep them clean and help them work more efficiently. Dirt and dust buildup insulate the coils so, as the air blows over them, less moisture is removed. The best way to clean the coils is to blow compressed air over them. You can buy spray cans of compressed air at a hardware store.

- **Regularly clean all areas prone to dampness**, such as the washing machine, dehumidifier, air conditioner, shower stalls, and the spaces around and under kitchen, bath, and laundry sinks; don't forget the refrigerator drip pan. Throw your dishrags in the laundry every day. Because bacteria and mildew flourish in damp toweling, hang towels and bath mats unfolded to hasten drying. In really humid weather, you should change towels and mats for fresh, dry replacements

at least every other day. (To reduce energy consumption, line dry towels—they'll smell fresher, too.) Clean the base of soap dishes in the shower and sink regularly, and keep shower curtains pulled shut to prevent dampness from collecting in the folds.

■ **Allergy-proof your vacuum.** Upgrade your machine by adding a superfine filter designed to catch tiny dust particles that regular filters miss. An increasing number of hardware stores and markets now carry allergy filters; if you can't find them there, order them from a supply company specializing in allergy-prevention products. A more expensive, but very effective, alternative is a vacuum with a high-efficiency particle absorbent (HEPA) filter.

TIP Making Cut Flowers Last

Change the water every day and avoid placing the flowers in direct sunlight. Add to the vase a little vodka, or bleach (a capful to a gallon of water), which will kill bacteria. Laundry detergent, which is the ingredient in those packets that your florist hands out, is also effective.

INNERWORKINGS

HVAC PROS AND CONS

You might think humankind had reached the zenith of comfort and convenience when someone invented an all-in-one air system that provides central heating, ventilating, and cooling (known by the acronym HVAC). Almost. An HVAC system certainly has many advantages. If you are having air-conditioning installed, using a single system of delivery for the cooled air (in summer) and heat (in winter) is cost-effective. You can also integrate a humidifier, air filters, and/or electronic air cleaners into such a system.

There are a few (minor) disadvantages as well. One is that an HVAC system is primarily designed to handle the air-conditioning component of the works, and the ducts are sized accordingly—which means they are bigger than they would be for an ordinary heating system. The reason is that an air-conditioning system has to move much more air to cool it than to warm it. In addition, a "compromise" is necessary in locating the registers. Air-conditioning outlets should be high in the wall or ceiling and heat outlets should be low in the wall or floor. Placing the ductwork and registers properly to deliver both heat and cool air is therefore a tricky balancing act.

OUTSIDE

- **Inspect walls and roof for mildew and moss**, particularly after a stretch of warm, damp weather. That greenish powder or slime you see clinging to siding and roof shingles is probably one of these annoying culprits. Clean the area by gently scrubbing with a bleach-and-water solution.

- **Maintain gutters and leaders**. After storms, check the gutters for debris and get it out before it clogs the works for the next rainstorm.

- **Be prepared for hurricanes and other storms that bring on whipping winds and damaging rains**. People living on the Gulf Coast or the Atlantic seaboard know (or should know) that they reside in the potential path of a hurricane. Summer and early fall are the seasons to prepare for these storms, as well as the summer tempests that can hit other parts of the country, including tropical storms from the Pacific. Start by replacing cracked windowpanes. If you live in a shore zone subject to seasonal storms, take the threat seriously. Invest in storm shutters or make simple versions from plywood. Secured with butterfly brackets, these can be easily installed when storm warnings are posted. It's also a good idea to stock up on plastic tarps, which you can use to protect furniture and electronic equipment in indoor areas that may leak.

- **Run a safety check after every summer storm**. Thunderstorms wreak havoc. Run your eye over electric and telephone wires to make sure they are free of any branches brought down by wind gusts and microbursts. Look above the wires for any hanging branches. Check foundations for signs of swelling or leaking, and make sure retaining walls aren't overstressed.

TIP Tornado Watch The frequency of tornadoes and microbursts seems to be increasing in many areas of the country including the Northeast, where we have had several bad windstorms in the last few years. When a tornado is coming, you must make life-or-death decisions quickly, so advance planning and fast response are essential. The Federal Emergency Management Agency recommends designating an area in your home as a shelter. Conduct drills and have flashlights, first-aid kits, and other disaster supplies on hand.

In any severe windstorm, open windows and doors to relieve pressure (if you have time). Move at once to a windowless interior room, storm cellar, or basement. If there is no basement, go to an inner hallway or a smaller inner room without windows, such as a bathroom or closet—any place where you can get away from windows. Go to the center of the room. Stay away from corners because they tend to attract debris. Get under a piece of sturdy furniture such as a workbench or heavy table or desk and hold on to it. If you are in a mobile home, get out and find shelter elsewhere.

After the storm, check for gas leaks. If you smell gas or hear a blowing or hissing noise, open the windows, leave quickly, and call the gas company from a neighbor's house. Look for electrical system damage: If you see sparks or frayed wires, turn off the electricity at the main fuse or circuit breaker.

GET SMART

OUTDOOR SECURITY

Although you should be concerned about security on your property throughout the year, summer is a good season to survey potential problems. For one thing, burglars favor summer months (and holidays) for break-ins; not only is it vacation season, but there's no snow on the ground to reveal footprints and other telltale tracks. Also at this time of year, trees, hedges, and bushes go through growth spurts; they should be trimmed near windows and doors to reduce potential cover for would-be intruders.

Walk around your house and look for tree branches that might give a burglar a leg up to windows, particularly at the back of the house and garage. If you are painting or doing other work that requires a ladder, resist the temptation to leave it leaning against the house overnight until the job is done. (And don't store a ladder by hanging it on the side of the garage.) Check the locks on all doors and basement and first- and second-story windows to make sure they are in working order. Do your entry doors swing in, rather than out, so that the hinges are mounted *inside?* For glass doors, I recommend key locks for outside *and* inside. Otherwise, an intruder can easily break the glass, reach in, and turn the dead bolt. Be sure a key is kept nearby. Slipping a wooden dowel into the bottom track on the inside of sliding doors also works.

Besides locking your garage and doors whenever you go out, you should also consider locking them when you are working in your yard. If this advice seems excessive, you might be surprised at how many houses are burgled by thieves who brazenly walk in while people are doing yard work or enjoying their swimming pools.

When you go away for extended periods, try to make your house look as though are you're there. Never let newspapers or mail collect. In summer, make sure someone continues to mow the lawn and handles yard work. In winter, have someone on call to shovel your walks and plow the driveway when it snows. Put your indoor lights on a timer and install outdoor lights with motion detectors by paths, entries, and stairs; the sensors, activated to turn lights on automatically when someone passes, are one of the best household crime preventers I know.

A final piece of advice: Call your local police force for a free security check (most offer this service and will send someone to inspect your property). And get to know your neighbors so you can keep an eye on one another. Neighbors who are familiar with your household patterns and routines are more likely to notice when something seems amiss. A friend of mine who lives at the end of a quiet country road has a neighbor about a quarter of a mile away who automatically looks to see whether he recognizes cars going to and from her house. She asks drivers to flash their headlights when they pass to signal that they are friends—if the lights don't flash, her neighbor checks the house to be sure all is well.

TIP Accessible Keys If you use an indoor/outdoor lock for glass doors, always keep a key handy. It should be near the door, and everyone in the family should know where to find it. In an emergency, you want to be able to get out quickly.

WEATHER VANES

A weather vane perched atop a house or barn has always seemed to me a quintessential symbol of American ingenuity and imagination: at once a handy meteorological instrument and a decorative work of folk art. Farmer and seafarer alike used vanes to determine wind direction from the early days of settlement in this country. An enormous range of forms proliferated, from the fish and ships favored in port towns to patriotic symbols (Lady Liberty and eagles) to cows, horses, sheep, and other farm animals. Many early weather vanes were produced by individual craftspeople, some of whom were well known as folk artists in their own time. Among the most commonly found examples today, however, are metal vanes (hammered over wooden molds) produced in factories from the mid- to late-1800s. Even then, a weather vane was a considerable investment, costing as much as $35—a hefty sum in the 19th century. If you have an old vane, check for a manufacturer's mark. Among the best-known firms making metal vanes in the 19th century were J. W. Fiske of New York and J. Howard and A. L. Jewell & Company, both of Massachusetts.

LIGHTNING RODS

According to the National Fire Protection Association, lightning strikes have caused an average of 8,500 structural fires annually over the last few years. The best protection from lightning is to install a system of terminals or rods that project above the roof. These lightning arresters, spaced at designated intervals and connected to one another by cables, are designed to transmit an electrical charge through cables to ground electrodes buried in the soil, where it can die a safe death. The idea is to offer the path of least resistance to the powerful surge of energy in a lightning strike. Because it is not a good conductor, a material like wood can be severely damaged in the process of resisting the electrical surge. On the other hand, metal materials on your house can attract lightning where you don't want it.

Separate structural elements—chimneys and roof cupolas, as well as television antennas, substantial roof flashing, copper gutters, and the like—must be protected with sizable lightning arresters as well. Always employ a professional for this job.

DECK, PORCH, AND Patio

- **Keep built-in planters and window boxes watered and fertilized.** Try not to allow the soil to dry out too much; it will be difficult to remoisten the plant thoroughly. Consider adding a water-retentive product to the potting mix to retain moisture.

- **Cool down paving surfaces.** You can drop the temperature underfoot by hosing down stone and concrete paving with cold water (try this poolside as well). The evaporation process will cool the surface, and the moisture will facilitate conduction of heat into the air and away from the ground.

- **Use plants to make a natural sun screen.** By high summer, you know where the hot spots are on your deck and patio. Potted trees and hanging plants, grouped or in a line, make great shade. Try hanging plants from hinged wall brackets that allow you to swing and re-position them. You can also install a trellis by your porch or deck and train shade-giving vines like wisteria or clematis to climb it. Around this time of year, many perennials start to go on sale at garden centers and it's actually a great time to plant, because the soil is warm. They won't flower this summer, but the roots will flourish and you'll have a healthy plant—and more shade—next summer, right where you want it.

- **Limit use of porch lights,** and use lanterns instead. Moths and

other bugs tend to congregate around lightbulbs, which is unattractive and particularly irritating when a fixture is located by patio or deck doors. In midsummer, I like to turn these lights off and substitute a flickering light from lanterns, torches, and paper-bag *luminarias* (great for parties). Tin or ceramic lanterns provide subtle light without attracting as many bugs.

TIP Planning Landscape Lighting A few judiciously placed spotlights can heighten drama and impress your guests. But plan carefully, with your outdoor living spaces in mind. When you are spotlighting shrubs and trees for nighttime effect, make sure to consider the view from porch, deck, or patio.

TIP Here Comes the Sun Among the many recent innovations in garden accents are solar-powered accessories. Small floating fountains and lights for patios, decks, and pathways (even floating lights for ponds) charge in the sunlight (for best results they need 48 hours of full sun), then turn on automatically.

HOME *A*LMANAC

GARAGE AND
*T*OOLSHED

■ **Storm-proof garage doors.** This is especially important if you live in a hurricane-prone area. You can purchase storm braces for garage doors at home supply outlets or install hurricane-rated garage doors.

■ **Ventilate work spaces frequently.** Ventilation is particularly important when you are using saws and sanders, as well as paints, stains, and glues, to prevent eye and throat irritation from dust and vapors. Consider installing an exhaust fan or a permanent dust-and-vapor collection system. Always keep skin covered as much as possible while you work.

■ **Install a tire bumper.** This should be bolted to the floor to catch your tire as you pull into the garage to park. You can buy one at a hardware or home supply store, or simply glue on a wood block with epoxy. In a narrow garage, protect the walls from opening car doors with a wall rail.

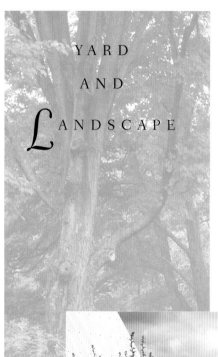

YARD
AND
$\mathcal{L}$ANDSCAPE

■ **Don't give up on weeding.** In the first bloom of summer, I actually enjoy waging war on weeds, particularly when they start to crowd out new, healthy annuals and perennials. So, weeding can be very satisfying. By the middle of July, I start to lose the incentive—it's hot, it's humid, and some of the flowers have finished blooming. Keep weeding anyway. Weeds flourish in midsummer and then can quickly take over.

■ **If you didn't mulch earlier, do it now.** A fresh layer of mulch gives your garden bed an amazing pick-me-up—it will help with the weed problem too. Another way to revive the look of flowerbeds is to rework the edges with an edging tool. Crisp up the existing edges or add a few curves for new interest.

■ **Water, water, water**—especially during heat waves and droughts. Lawn, flowers, and vegetable beds would all profit from at least an inch of water weekly, but water use may be limited during drought periods. Water in the morning or late afternoon because when the sun is

high, some of the moisture will evaporate before it gets where it is needed. Grass can get burned by reflected sunlight, and watering at high noon can actually create brown patches of lawn.

- **Deadhead annuals and perennials.** Trimming dead blossoms helps the plant maximize energy. You'll get more blooms from annuals, and you will encourage continued blooming from certain perennials.

- **Fill in with annuals.** It's not too late to plant. Add salvia, marigolds, zinnias, cosmos, and other varieties to provide extra cutting flowers and add color in spots where early-blooming perennials have gone by. New annuals can also refresh container arrangements.

- **Stake tall plants**. Hollyhocks, delphiniums, and other tall flowers are especially vulnerable to the high winds and heavy rains of summer storms. So are tomato plants. If you haven't staked them yet, do so now.

- **Prune maples, birches, lindens, horse chestnuts,** and other varieties that continue to produce sap during their spring growing season. By July, growth has slowed enough to make this a good time for trimming.

TIP Irises July and August, just after the blooming period is over, are a great time to plant irises. Plant the tall bearded varieties that will benefit from getting their roots well established before the growing season ends. Mail-order suppliers offer an incredible selection; you can order from catalogues now and keep planting right into September. Irises prefer a sunny spot in a well-drained, well-weeded bed. Plant them with the roots spread out downward and the tops of the rhizomes skimming the soil so that they are exposed to the sun.

TIP Organic Pest Repellents
An easy repellent to make is a natural solution of concentrated lemon that combats insects with citric acid. Ants, aphids, cabbage loopers, mealybugs, slugs, and whiteflies all hate it. To get rid of moles, try a castor oil–based repellent. Use garlic clips or Millorgonite (an organic fertilizer) to deter deer.

INSIDE

- Keep dander down and allergens at bay.
- Make sure ceiling fans are working properly.
- Try some all-natural home-care products.
- Clean your dehumidifier (again)!
- Clean window balances.

OUTSIDE

- Touch up exterior paint.
- Repair broken or cracked window glass.
- Adjust doors and hardware.

DECK, PORCH, AND PATIO

- Clean the barbecue grill.
- Take care of outdoor furniture.
- Maintain and rearrange your outdoor furniture.
- Turn off indoor lights when you're outside.

GARAGE AND TOOLSHED

- Recycle bags for garbage.
- Clean your garbage pails.

YARD AND LANDSCAPE

- Look for bargains at garden centers.
- Order bulbs for fall planting.
- Collect seeds.
- Direct-seed for fall vegetable crops.
- Water the lawn.

August

I'm remembering school days, when the approach of Labor Day heralded the end of summer vacation and impending doom. In any case, I have mixed feelings about August. Even when the dog days arrive in July, and I find myself tinkering in my workshop in an admittedly desultory way, I mourn the end of the season. On the other hand, when those few crisp, effortless days set in near the end of the month, I suddenly feel rejuvenated, and new ideas for projects inside and out begin to flow.

■ **Keep dander down and allergens at bay.** Two effective strategies are to wash your sheets in the hottest water that's safe for them and to enclose feather pillows in a zipper cloth case before putting on the pillow cases. You can also purchase "allergy-proof" covers for mattresses, pillows, and quilts. Damp-wipe window blinds and fan blades and vacuum your home thoroughly at least once a week. Consider removing any heavy or high-pile rugs for the rest of the season and putting away your kids' stuffed animals.

■ **Make sure ceiling fans are working properly.** If a fan develops an annoying vibration, check for a warped blade, loose blade screws, or a wobbling motor. Clean the blades regularly.

■ **Try some all-natural home-care products.** The chemical content of cleansers can be particularly irritating in humid weather, when fumes lodge in draperies and carpeting. Look for nontoxic ingredients, such as linseed oil, carnauba wax, and bergamot oil on product labels. Opt for a fragrance-free all-purpose cleanser and a citrus-infused paste wax.

■ **Clean your dehumidifier (again)!** These machines really need to be cleaned at least twice during the high summer season. Make sure that the coils are thoroughly dry before cleaning them, and wipe any slime or film from the basin.

■ **Clean window balances.**
Humid summer weather can mean sticky double-hung windows. Sometimes the problem is caused by swelling wood, but checking and cleaning the *balances*, the tracks in which the sash slides up and down, is a good idea. Whether they're made of wood, plastic, aluminum, or another metal, they can all be cleaned with mild detergent. If necessary, lubricate the tracks with silicone spray—not oil, which can build up and trap dirt—but only if the window really drags. You don't want to over-lubricate, because most balances require only a little friction to hold the window partly or completely open. If you aren't sure what type or style of window you have, consult a handyman or ask at your local hardware store. You may even be lucky (or unlucky) enough to have old windows with *real* balances: a system of ropes, cast-iron weights, and pulleys that actually balance the window as it moves up and down the frame. The tracks in newer windows perform the same balancing act, holding the sash in place wherever it stops; this is the reason the tracks are now called balances.

SAFETY FIRST

ALARM SYSTEMS

For home care, an electronic security system is one of the best investments you can make. Alarm systems come in many incarnations and in different levels of sophistication and complexity. The individual needs of the homeowner dictate the choice out of the three basic types; not all are necessary for everyone. One is the fire alarm, which sounds an alert and notifies a monitoring station to dial the fire department when smoke and/or high heat is detected. The second is a security system, which sounds an alarm and notifies the monitoring station to call the police (or whomever else you designate) if your house security is breached. The third is an emergency system, which can be a panic button that instantly summons help in a fire, police, or medical emergency.

For each type of system, the many options to consider are too numerous to list. Among the most common are window and door trip buttons, motion detectors, temperature sensors, carbon-monoxide detectors, glass-breaking sensors, smoke alarms, and heat detectors. The systems can dial for emergency services, sound an alarm inside and outside, blink your lights, shout a taped warning, notify you or your grandmother if the pipes are freezing in the family ski lodge, or detect someone driving down your driveway.

Any such system should be installed by one of the many professional companies that sell alarms. To locate a good one, request a referral from someone you trust. I have found that most of these firms are very good, but their products and services can vary greatly in cost. Shop for price, service, and reliability and get several quotes—not just for price, but for your specific needs. A good alarm company will help you sort through all the options. Remember that in addition to the cost of purchase and installation, there is a fee, usually billed quarterly, to monitor the system and respond to problems and emergencies.

DRYING FLOWERS NATURALLY

Drying flowers successfully starts with the picking. Whether you gather plants from fields, roadside, or your own garden beds, the best bet is to snip flowers just before they peak. Fuller blooms are more likely to drop off as the plants dry. Some loss is inevitable, so if you are considering a specific project, such as making a wreath, gather and preserve more flowers than you think are required. Throughout the summer, I cut and preserve flowers as I pick them. By August I pay particular attention to lush late-season bloomers like purple coneflower, sedum, and certain herbs, like mint and thyme, that are taking over the garden. At this time of year, you can also collect Queen Anne's lace, seed pods, rose hips, berries, and leaves. If you live in the Northeast, watch for the striking colors of sugar maples and staghorn sumac.

The easiest natural method for preserving flowers is to air-dry them in a warm, dark, well-ventilated place, where you can hang the plants—typically the attic or a closet. Don't use the kitchen because moisture and grease from cooking will spoil the process. When you cut stems for drying, strip off some of the lower leaves while the plants are still fresh to avoid trapping moisture that will cause rot and mildew. Bunch flowers gently together in like kinds, gathering as many as you can bunch easily without crushing the leaves or stems. Be sure to stagger the blossoms and loosen the stems so that air can circulate. Snag the stems near the bottom with a rubber band, then hang them upside down on a string. If you have limited hanging space, put the flowers in paper bags and store them in a dry place. To prevent damaging flowers with large, flat blossoms, such as daisies and Queen Anne's lace, you can also try spreading them out on a screen or other meshed surface that is suspended horizontally above the floor so air can circulate (rest the screen ends on a couple of chairs or boxes). I've even had luck drying sturdy stems of pods and leaves by sticking them upright in an umbrella stand.

Drying time varies from two to six weeks, depending on the type of plant. No matter what the method, plants must be stored in a dry area and kept away from light to prevent fading. A little fading is inevitable, so keep some substitutes on hand. Be sure all materials are absolutely dry before using them.

OUTSIDE

■ **Touch up exterior paint.** If you haven't undertaken a major paint job, try to do any necessary touch-ups before fall sets in. If you wait until too late in the fall, a sudden drop in temperature can compromise your paint job. Scrape, sand, and clean any areas that are bare, blistered, or peeling to prepare the surface. Spot prime as needed and then apply a finish coat with enough overlap to adhere to the existing paint surface.

■ **Repair broken or cracked window glass.** Fixing broken windowpanes held in place with glazing compound (a special putty used to install glass) takes a little practice but is basically an easy task. The process typically involves removing old putty with a putty knife or chisel, applying a fresh bed of glazing compound, and then installing a new piece of glass. If the repair seems too complicated, any hardware store or glass retailer will do the job for you or help with some advice.

It's easy—and a good idea—to remove the broken glass in the meantime, particularly if there are jagged edges. Use pliers to pull out the glass gently. You'll also need to use a putty knife to extract the small metal triangular "points" that hold it in the sash. Some windowpanes are held in by wood molding fitted with small brads; you must take these out as well. In a metal window frame (such as aluminum), a vinyl gasket usually holds in the glass; this should also be pulled out.

■ **Adjust doors and hardware.**
Check hinges, knobs, screws, and strikes to be sure they are tight and work as they should. Avoid using oil on any exterior (or exposed) knobs and hinges; they can clog up and get gummy later in the winter when the temperature is colder. In the summer heat and humidity, exterior doors swell up and may need some adjusting or planing to work more easily. If a door is really swollen, you may need to take it off its hinges and trim it slightly with a plane. But take care not to over trim because it will likely be too loose in the winter when it shrinks back to its "dry size." As always, call a carpenter if you are unsure about how to do this job yourself.

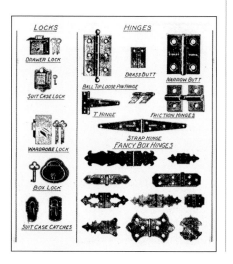

GET SMART

SUN SENSE

By now we all know that too much sun can be unhealthy. Even when it is filtered through glass, sunlight damages virtually anything because it delivers both heat and ultraviolet rays. The heat dries out most materials and shortens their life by causing brittleness and fading. Ultraviolet light is a sub ray of sunlight that breaks down the fibers of practically all materials except gold, silver, and platinum. Wood, cloth, paint, shingles, blacktop, fabrics, and human skin are all susceptible.

The best way to combat the effect of ultraviolet degeneration is to reduce exposure to sunlight. Plant trees, install awnings on windows and porches, and use the best possible grades of exterior paint, stains, shingles, and other sheathing materials. Wood shingles can be protected with sun-blocking sealers, and asphalt and fiberglass roof shingles are typically embedded with tiny stone granules to reflect light (the reason they seem to glitter). This enables the shingles to withstand the constant exposure to sun and the resulting UV degradation. Shades and curtains help shield the furnishings inside your home from the harmful rays that travel through unprotected window glass. It's still a good idea, however, to choose window glass coated with a UV-blocking film or to buy windows manufactured specifically for UV protection.

DECK, PORCH, AND $\mathcal{P}$ATIO

■ **Clean the barbecue grill.** If you haven't been cleaning the grill all summer, do it now. By this time, plenty of grease, soot, and old food will have collected. Run a gas grill for 10 to 15 minutes on high to burn off residue, then turn off the flame and clean with a wire brush while the rack is still warm. To clean a charcoal grill rack, leave the rack over the hot coals for 20 minutes after cooking, remove it with protective gloves, and clean it with a wire brush. If you are still having trouble removing the grime, let the rack cool and go at it with a steel-wool soap pad. After each use, clean out the charcoal ash and catch pan when the coals are thoroughly cooled and make sure the vents are clear.

■ **Maintain and rearrange your outdoor furniture.** A good cleaning solution for white-resin patio furniture is 3/4 cup household bleach and 1 tablespoon powder or liquid laundry detergent to a gallon of water. Apply the mixture to a small area with a sponge and let it stand for five minutes. Then scrub with a soft brush and rinse, working your way over the entire piece. This solution can remove mildew and will get most resin furniture clean and white again (always spot-test first.) There are also commercial products on the market specifically recommended for use on outdoor furniture.

Keep rearranging your porch and garden furniture. If you keep shifting furniture arrangements to follow the sun and shade, you'll find that you can significantly stretch the daylight hours when patios and decks are pleasant to use. As days shorten in the fall, this is a good way to extend the use of outdoor spaces.

■ **Turn off indoor lights when you're using your deck, porch, or patio at night.** Otherwise, insects will paste themselves over French doors and glass sliders, and it's impossible to keep them out of the house when you go in or out.

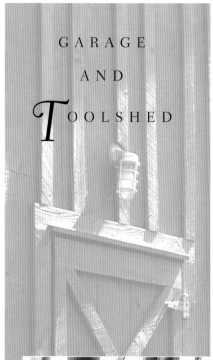

GARAGE AND
T OOLSHED

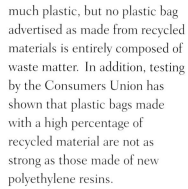

■ **Recycle bags for garbage.** As recently as 30 years ago, none of us had ever heard of a plastic garbage bag. According to the Environmental Protection Agency, plastic bag waste now takes up more than 2 percent of all dump and landfill space in the United States. Several years ago, manufacturers answered environmental concerns with so-called biodegradable products, but the Federal Trade Commission challenged the companies' unsubstantiated degradability claims. Now manufacturers use recycled waste plastic to deflect criticism about the use of too much plastic, but no plastic bag advertised as made from recycled materials is entirely composed of waste matter. In addition, testing by the Consumers Union has shown that plastic bags made with a high percentage of recycled material are not as strong as those made of new polyethylene resins.

I still think the best option is real recycling; rather than buying new bags (of recycled material or not), use shopping bags saved from grocery and other stores and limit the use of new plastic bags to the large liners in your outside garbage pails.

■ **Clean your garbage pails.** Even if you use large plastic garbage bags, something always seems to stick to garbage cans. When grime builds up, it becomes gummy and impossible to get out. What's more, old food and trash attract rodents, insects, mold, and bacteria, which really fester in late summer humidity. Take your garbage cans outside, remove the covers, and wash them down with disinfectant. Rinse them with a garden hose, and be sure to dry them thoroughly to prevent mildew or stagnant water, which attracts insects.

HOME *A*LMANAC

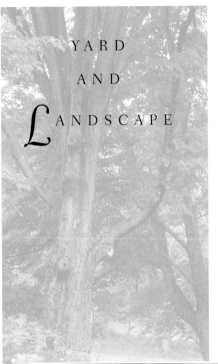

YARD
AND
*L*ANDSCAPE

■ **Look for bargains at garden centers.** At this time of year, garden centers offer great buys on both annuals and perennials. Last August, I got five or six flats of snapdragons at half price and created an instant cottage garden by my back door. They were perfect—fuller, straighter, and taller than I ever would have grown them myself (snaps always seem to grow sideways in my garden).

■ **Order bulbs for fall planting.** You can always buy daffodils, crocuses, and other bulbs that require fall planting at your garden center later in autumn, but I prefer ordering by mail now. Catalogues give you a broad range of options while offering design ideas for mixing colors and varieties. What's more, buying in bulk by mail usually affords customers a discount. Every year I split one large order with a friend, and we both save money.

■ **Collect seeds.** Late summer, as blossoms and seed heads brown and pods appear, is the time to harvest seeds from fruit, vegetables, and flowers for next year's garden. Seed heads snipped off the plant and stored in a closed paper bag, in a warm, dry place, will conveniently drop their seeds when you shake the bag after drying for a couple of weeks. Collect the seeds in a paper envelope and save some for Christmas presents. When gathering seeds from fleshy fruits or vegetables such as cucumbers or squash, scoop them out with your fingers or a spoon. Rinse the seeds in tepid water and blot them dry with absorbent paper towels. To dry them thoroughly, tuck them into a plastic bag with some dry cornmeal and refrigerate over the winter.

■ **Direct-seed for fall vegetable crops.** It's not too late for turnips, winter squash, and pumpkins. Meanwhile, keep harvesting late vegetables such as peppers before the first frost.

■ **Water the lawn.** In my neck of the woods, August is drought season; water twice a week if rain is scarce. If you use an oscillating sprinkler on the grass, you won't have to move the sprinkler head as often. Watering early in the evening permits the grass to absorb moisture throughout the night. Or water early in the morning; if you water during the strong sunlight hours, much of the moisture will be lost to evaporation.

THINGS TO DO IN SEPTEMBER

INSIDE

- Get your woodstove in working order.
- Have your heating system evaluated.
- Check to see if radiators need bleeding.
- Inspect chimney flues.
- Check your fireplace dampers.

OUTSIDE

- Stock firewood.
- Do some chimney maintenance.
- Make sure your chimney cap is secure.
- Check for rodent entry points.

DECK, PORCH, AND PATIO

- Bring potted plants indoors.
- Clean efflorescence from patio pavers.

GARAGE AND TOOLSHED

- Weather-strip your garage door.
- Dispose of toxic paints and chemical substances.

YARD AND LANDSCAPE

- Keep weeding.
- Plant shrubs and trees.
- Start cutting back perennials.
- De-thatch and aerate grass.
- Keep mowing.
- Harvest the last of your summer herbs and vegetables.
- Attempt some deer-proofing.

September

As I write this, it's late in September. Looking out my window, I can see, of all things, a hot air balloon floating into view above a line of maple trees just starting to tinge red around the edges. The balloon seems the right symbol for a month that brings high spirits and a fresh start. Though some people might be duped into believing that January is the beginning of the year, others of us know the calendar really starts with September. And what could put fall energy to better use than some projects around the house?

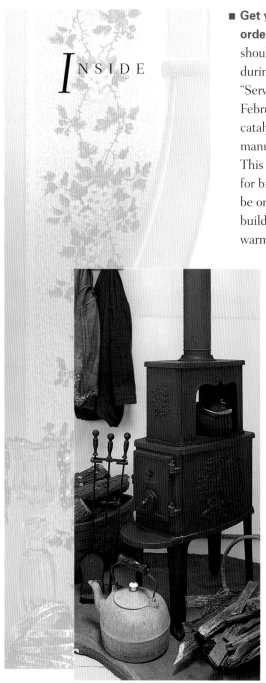

I NSIDE

■ **Get your woodstove in working order.** Wood-burning stoves should be cleaned several times during the heating season (see "Service Your Woodstove," February). If the stove has a catalytic combuster, check the manual for cleaning instructions. This is also a good time to inspect for birds' nests in the chimney and be on the lookout for creosote buildup. If the past winter was warm, you may have choked the stove down to burn slower fires. Limiting air flow, however, can increase creosote deposits, so don't forgo a cleaning because you think that you've underused your stove the previous season.

■ **Have your heating system evaluated.** Once a year, a plumber or licensed heating contractor can adjust burners, monitor the pressure of a hot-water system, tune up a blower or heat-pump motor, check ducts for leaks, replace the fan belt, and clean or replace air and other filters. This process should include a long list of safety checks performed by the professional. The goal is to make sure that the system is using fuel as efficiently and safely as possible while distributing heat evenly. Like a car or any appliance, a heating system will last longer and have fewer problems if it's kept tuned and serviced.

■ **Check to see if radiators need bleeding.** Sooner or later air is bound to build up in your hot-water heating system. This means the system will work less efficiently because air is a poor heat conductor. Most modern boilers have automatic bleeders, but while these minimize problems, they don't eliminate them completely. The need to bleed may be indicated by a radiator that clanks or doesn't seem to heat. If you have a hot-water system and can hear water running through the pipes, there is probably some air in the lines. You can bleed the air out by using a radiator key or screwdriver to turn the bleed valve (about a quarter turn). Hold it open until the hissing stops and the water flows steadily without spurting. Start with the radiator closest to the boiler. (If you don't want to do this

HOME *A* LMANAC

yourself, just call your plumber.) If you have a hot-air system, check and clean the filters and vacuum the registers.

TIP Clean Glass The Chimney Safety Institute of America suggests cleaning glass woodstove doors with a crumpled piece of damp newspaper dipped in fine wood ash. Wipe in a circular motion.

- **Inspect chimney flues.** A clogged chimney can contribute to the threat of carbon monoxide poisoning, particularly in a "tight" house. Another potential problem is a chimney fire, which can be ignited by burning creosote. Creosote, a residue, is caused by poor air flow, a cooler-than-normal chimney, and smoke from unseasoned firewood. The high temperature of chimney fires can break down the mortar, crack tiles, and collapse the flue (an interior clay pipe that funnels smoke and fumes out the chimney), damaging exterior masonry. Metal chimneys will buckle, warp, or split their seams under the high temperatures.

  A licensed chimney sweep can check for these problems and for cracks and other damage from frost, snow, ice, wind, and lightning. Having a pro check your chimney is especially important if it does not have a flue, which is often the case in older homes. A flueless chimney is harder to keep clean and likely to smoke into the house or attic. In lieu of rebuilding the chimney to add a flue, a liner can be installed.

- **Check your fireplace dampers.** A damper is a small door that leads from your fireplace interior to the chimney. In most cases, the damper is best kept closed when the fireplace is not in use to prevent cold air from entering your house through the chimney. During a bad storm, a gust of wind can actually send ashes and soot flying into the room. Be sure that the damper is in working order and that it opens and closes easily. If it is stuck in one place or covered with rust, you should get it fixed or replaced.

UNDERSTANDING HEATING SYSTEMS

Home heating systems can be fueled by a variety of energy sources ranging from wood to the sun, but your system probably runs on one of the more common types of fuel or energy—gas, oil, or electricity. The fuel operates a type of system that heats your home in a particular way— usually by means of forced air (blown through registers), hot water or steam (heating baseboard heaters and radiators), or electric baseboard heaters.

In a *forced-air system*, the air is heated by a *furnace*, which may run on oil, gas, or in some cases wood. A blower carries the warmed air through a system of ducts feeding adjustable grates or registers in each room. A *heat pump* is a common component of forced-

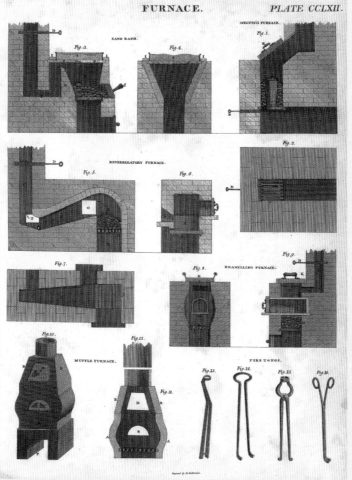

FURNACE.   *PLATE CCLXII.*

air systems. In a *heat-pump* system, the pump is designed to collect some warmth from the outside air and send it indoors—in much the same way that a central air-conditioning system collects the heat from the warm air inside and pumps it outside. (In fact, a central air-conditioning unit technically *is* a heat pump.) No matter how cold it is outside, there is always some heat in the air; but when the air is too cold for this process to be efficient, the main heating system takes over entirely from the pump or supplements the warm air.

In a *hot-water system*, water is heated in a *boiler*, then piped to the radiators or baseboard heaters, and back again to the boiler in a constant cycle. The water moves via circulating pumps from the boiler to the rest of the house. The boiler usually runs on gas or oil, and wood-burning boilers are also available. In a *steam system*, the boiler vaporizes hot water into pressurized steam, which is also piped to radiators. A steam gauge makes it possible to check the safety range of the steam pressure. Excess pressure is vented by means of a safety valve.

In an *electric system*, radiant heat is generated in baseboard convectors or by embedded floor or ceiling cables. Electric heating is clean and easy to run and maintain, but expensive to operate.

In an *HVAC system*, heating and air-conditioning are delivered by the same duct system (see "HVAC Pros and Cons," July).

Heating systems are regulated by *thermostats*, which allow you to set the desired air temperature. When it is reached, the heating system automatically turns off. If the temperature drops below the designated level, the system restarts and runs until the set level is reached again—which is why you hear the boiler or furnace cranking up repeatedly throughout the day or during the night.

Any heating system can be set up by thermostats governing *zones,* so you can regulate the heat in different rooms (or even different areas of the same room) according to use. Multiple zones can be efficient in burning fuel, but such a system is usually costly to install because it requires individual controls and piping or ductwork and circulation systems for each zone.

Should you turn the thermostat down at night and when you're away from home or leave it at the same level? The answer depends on the size of the space and the length of time. You can waste a lot of fuel heating the space back up, particularly if you are resetting the thermostat several times a day. On the other hand, if you're going away for at least two or three days, you can set the temperature at a lower level, because the cost of cranking the system back up will be less than the amount you can save in oil costs over this longer period. Turning down the setting by five degrees or so is fine at night.

Remember that all thermostats are not created equal. Location is an important factor: If the thermostat is positioned five feet above the floor on an inside wall, as most should be, it reads the temperature *at that location*. If your home is old or drafty, don't set your thermostats too low when you go away: The air at floor level on the house exterior and in closets or "dead" areas with little air circulation can get very cold, even causing pipes to freeze.

TIP Cold Air Return? Does the air blowing through the heating registers in your home feel cold rather than warm? To heat a room to 70°F, the hot-air system may be blowing in air that is 75°F. Because the air temperature is much lower than the temperature of your skin, the air feels cold even though the room is heated to 70°F.

LINKS TO THE PAST

CHIMNEY SWEEPS

Formalized as a trade in the Georgian period, chimney cleaning had developed into a thriving profession in England by the Victorian era, coinciding with the spread of coal as a heating fuel. By the mid-1800s, more than a thousand sweeps are said to have been at work in London, where smoke and cinders from coal fires blackened the skyline, coated buildings with a grimy residue, and dramatically increased the risk of chimney fires.

Like most trades, chimney cleaning was learned by apprenticeship to a master. In this case, however, the dangerous job fell to small boys, who were required to climb inside the chimney flues and clean them by hand. Many of these apprentices, who received training in exchange for their room and board, were sold into the trade from orphanages for a period of indentured servitude. According to rules set by the London Society of Master Sweeps, the apprentices worked six days a week and were required to attend Sunday school on their day off to learn to read the Bible.

An 1864 act of Parliament made forcing children

to climb inside chimneys illegal, but before this date virtually no regulations protected young chimney sweeps from the many hazards of their trade. Even before this legislation, however, there were alternatives to putting a human cleaner in the chimney flue. One cleaning method involved lowering a brush down the chimney with a weighted ball. Another employed a system of flexible canes and whalebone brushes that could be worked up the chimney interior from the hearth.

Technology be praised: You don't need a Dickensian street urchin to clean your chimney. After an initial visual inspection, a modern chimney sweep will likely use a video camera to determine whether there are problems. Most professionals work from the opening of the fireplace and clean with a large commercial vacuum. You can find a certified chimney sweep (also called a chimney technician) by looking in the Yellow Pages; for more information contact the National Chimney Sweep Guild or the Chimney Safety Institute of America.

OUTSIDE

■ **Stock firewood.** Cordwood should be stored outdoors in a protected area or a woodshed—not in your basement or garage. Ideally, you want a mix of hardwoods, which pound for pound have about double the heating capacity of the much less dense softwoods. Hardwoods give off more heat, with fewer flames and less sparking, and burn longer and hotter. Resinous pines and other softwoods are likely to produce creosote because they burn faster and cooler, and should be avoided. Oak is one of the best firewoods; other good woods for burning include ash, aspen, birch, hickory, and maple. Whatever the choice, firewood should be split and well dried. Don't burn construction scraps or wood that has been painted, varnished, or treated in any way.

■ **Do some chimney maintenance.** This job is not limited to the indoors. Climb a ladder and survey the flashing around the base of the chimney where it enters the roof for signs of leaking. Flashings are intended to keep rain and melting snow from getting into the house. You can test for leaks with a garden hose. If you have a metal chimney pipe, be alert to rust and scrape it off with a wire brush. Prime and paint with products recommended for the job.

Check for signs of past chimney fires, like cracks in the exterior masonry and smoke smudges around the mortar joints. (Slow-

burning chimney fires can go undetected before burning themselves out.) If you think a fire may have occurred, call a certified chimney sweep.

- **Make sure your chimney cap is secure.** If you don't have a cap, consider installing one. Fitted with mesh inserts, these metal covers are designed to prevent cinders from landing on the roof and help keep damaging rain out of the chimney stack. Water mixing with creosote can become acidic and rust the damper, damage the flue, or pit mortar joints. A chimney cap also keeps out birds and nesting animals.

- **Check for rodent entry points.** In fall and winter you need to worry about infestation, because this is when mice and red squirrels come inside in search of warmth, food, and shelter. A mouse, especially a small or young one, can wriggle

through the smallest of holes. The foundation is the first area to inspect, but mice can climb all the way up to the roof to get in. Check the area where the chimney meets the roof and look for holes under the roof eaves.

Cracks in masonry and cement should be patched with mortar. Small holes can also be stuffed with steel wool. In some cases, wire cloth, also known as hardware cloth, is a good solution for exterior exhaust vents that can't be fully covered (like the one for your clothes dryer) and attract mice with their heat. The mesh should have a ⅜-inch gauge (no more), or rodents will get in. Keep an eye on any vent that expels warm air (from your stove, for instance).

TIP Measuring Cordwood Firewood is typically sold in a unit known as a cord (hence the term *cordwood*), which is measured as a pile exactly 4 feet wide and deep and 8 feet long (128 cubic feet). A "face cord" is 4 feet wide by 8 feet long, but only as deep as the length of a single log. A face cord of 16-inch wood is one third of a cord.

FIREWOOD WISDOM

A safe, efficiently burning fire in your woodstove or fireplace depends on dry, split, well-seasoned fuel to ensure a good draft. The key word is *dry*. The wetter the wood, the harder it is to ignite, and the greater the heat loss when it does burn. Because it burns a smoky, cooler fire than dry wood, unseasoned, or "green," wood contributes to ash and creosote buildup in your chimney. When buying cordwood, be sure to ask whether it is seasoned. If you are collecting or cutting your own, set it aside to dry out for at least six months to a year (unrotted deadfall can be burned right away). A well-seasoned piece of wood shows cracks on the cut face and makes a crisp pinging noise when banged against another log. No cracks and a dull, thudding sound indicate green or rotten wood.

Stacking wood properly means keeping it dry and ensuring maximum air circulation. One objective is to keep logs off the ground so that air can get under them. Use shims, a storage pallet, or a few pieces of wood to keep your stack from resting directly on the damp ground. When stacking wood, alternate the direction of each layer lengthwise and crosswise to create air pockets, and if possible, orient the stack to catch the sun and prevailing breezes. Keep the wood away from roof eaves or overhanging tree branches that might direct rain water and snow onto it. If you cover the stack with a tarp, be sure it is loose enough to allow moisture to escape and air to circulate.

I always warn against storing wood in your garage or basement because you're creating a nice, warm condominium complex for a full range of critters, including spiders, carpenter ants, powder-post beetles, mice, and termites. The risk is even greater if the wood is deadfall, because some creature has probably already taken up residence. Logs piled against the house are a magnet for insects and rodents that can work their way indoors. The best option is a woodshed, where you can store and season your wood.

DECK, PORCH, AND *P*ATIO

■ **Bring potted plants indoors.**
Unless you live in the South or
Southwest, your outdoor container
plants don't have much time left.
Some potted annuals won't make
it indoors, where they often
succumb to pests that don't
bother them during their natural
course of life outdoors. However,
I always have luck with
geraniums, which can be wintered
successfully inside if you put
them in a sunny spot and water
and feed them regularly.

■ **Clean efflorescence from patio
pavers.** The chalky white film
known as efflorescence appears
on many types of pavers—
including those made of
concrete, brick, and
some types of stone.
This film is calcium
carbonate, which forms
when lime or calcium
oxide in the paving
materials gets wet and
reacts with carbon
dioxide in the air. The
white coating appears
when the pavers are dry
and is less visible when
they're wet. To remove
it try rubbing with a
stiff brush and soapy
water. If this doesn't
work, use a solution of
muriatic acid (sold at
hardware stores) and
water (1 part acid to
20 parts water)
or a commercial
efflorescence-cleaning
solution made
specifically for masonry.

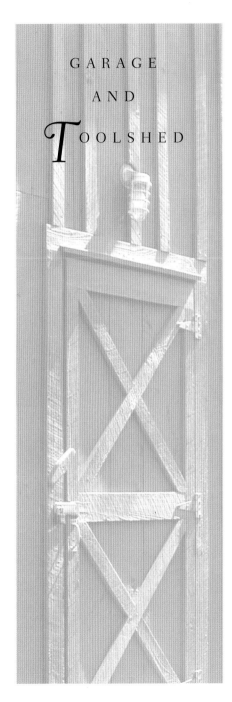

GARAGE
AND
T OOLSHED

- **Weather-strip your garage door.** Using a vinyl weather stripping designed for this purpose helps keep mice and cold air out.

- **Dispose of toxic paints and chemical substances** that you might be storing in your garage or a utility shed. Ideally, you should tackle this twice a year, but if you are going to do it once, this is the time. Strict regulations make it illegal to dispose of alkyd-based paint, pesticides, and other substances containing poisons except under very supervised conditions. Therefore you can't just throw a can of old oil paint into your garbage or even take it to the dump. Most municipalities schedule periodic toxic dumping days, usually at the local landfill, and these days are often Saturdays in September. At these times, you are permitted to bring any dangerous materials to the designated site, usually free of charge. Check at your town hall for a schedule.

YARD AND LANDSCAPE

- **Keep weeding.** Don't be fooled into thinking that weeds sprouting in the fall won't survive the winter. Some, like chickweed, do, only to return in full force the next spring. Get rid of weeds now.

- **Plant shrubs and trees.** Recent research shows that the best planting season for most tree species other than evergreens is fall, partly because the soil is in better condition for digging. By the next spring, roots are settled into place and are better able to soak up moisture on their own. Water new trees and shrubs thoroughly at least once a week with a slow-flowing hose to soak the roots, which will keep growing until the ground temperature falls to about 50° F.

- **Start cutting back perennials.** Begin with those fading plants that have large leaves to prevent rot, which attracts pests and promotes mold. Now is also the time to divide many types of perennials, including daylilies and phlox.

- **De-thatch and aerate grass.** It's a good idea to get rid of the rotting grass stems and other natural debris, or thatch, that builds up on your lawn over the summer. Left alone, it promotes weed growth and insect infestation. Aerating the soil, or loosening the dirt (which gets compressed by repeated mowing), is designed to let air circulate so that the roots of grass can breathe. Do the job with an aerating rake or lawn mower attachment or rent an aerating machine from a hardware store or garden center.

TIP Fall Is Bargain Season

At this time of year, shrubs and small trees can be marked down as much as 50 percent. Plants put in now will benefit from warm soil, but they may not look as good when you buy them as they do in the spring. Because the plants have been waiting around to be bought for several months, don't expect a perfect specimen. Just check that the roots are healthy and the foliage is in generally good shape. Deciduous shrubs may already be dropping their leaves, but that doesn't matter.

- **Keep mowing.** When cooler temperatures arrive in early fall, your grass will go through a post-drought growth spurt. Don't be fooled into thinking the mowing season is over.

- **Harvest the last of your summer herbs and vegetables before the first frost.** Basil, for one, won't survive a light frost, so pick it for pesto before your crop gets wasted. Whole basil leaves freeze well for future use in plastic bags, but freezing pesto in ice trays works well, too—you can pop out the number of cubes you need for each meal. Hardier herbs like rosemary can be transplanted to pots for window gardens indoors.

- **Attempt some deer-proofing.** Depending on where you live, deer may be a problem all year long (see "Keeping Out Deer," June). I raise the subject now, however, because many homeowners are most troubled by these marauding animals in the fall and winter. As grazing opportunities diminish, deer munch on yews, junipers, and other shrubs. Because you and your pets are probably spending much less time outdoors around your house, there is also less activity to scare deer away.

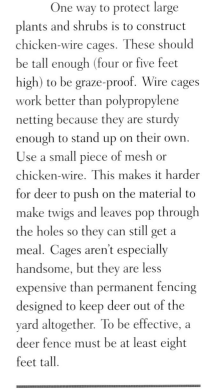

One way to protect large plants and shrubs is to construct chicken-wire cages. These should be tall enough (four or five feet high) to be graze-proof. Wire cages work better than polypropylene netting because they are sturdy enough to stand up on their own. Use a small piece of mesh or chicken-wire. This makes it harder for deer to push on the material to make twigs and leaves pop through the holes so they can still get a meal. Cages aren't especially handsome, but they are less expensive than permanent fencing designed to keep deer out of the yard altogether. To be effective, a deer fence must be at least eight feet tall.

TIP The Root of the Matter

A tree-planting hole should be cone-shaped, with the deepest part at the center because roots tend to grow horizontally and near the surface. Don't dig out too much: Make the hole diameter no more than three times that of the root ball. Use a fertilizer with a high phosphorus content to stimulate root growth rather than one with a high nitrogen content, which will make leaves grow.

FALL

Thinking of fall, I picture my grandmother's cold cellar. In a cool corner at the north end of the basement, she put up innumerable canning jars filled with peaches, tomatoes, beets, and pickled cucumbers. I remember watching her blanch the fruits and vegetables in scalding water and rim the jars with rubber gaskets; the homemade jams and jellies were often sealed with paraffin. When my grandmother asked me to get her something from that cellar, I considered it an adventure. I pushed open the pine door to marvel at the array of colored glass jars lined up as neatly as in a general store. The shelves held baskets of apples, and butternut squash sat next to large blue Hubbards. Such memories are a valued part of my past, when my family members lived near or with one another and interacted daily. It was a time when passing on knowledge and experience from one generation to the next meant learning by actually doing.

Remembering these rituals, I always see fall as a time of transitions. The endings and beginnings of many of our home experiences seem to happen during this season, when we are all busy. The urgency we feel about winter preparations stems from an era when the need for them was very real. Although few of us need to do our own canning, simple rituals like putting up preserves are entrenched in the patterns of the season because they still give us so much pleasure. Now I think of harvesting late vegetables—like pumpkins, acorn squash, and Brussels sprouts—before putting the gardens to bed for the winter. I remember my grandfather working the remaining plants into the soil with a spade while I crawled ahead of him seeking the last fruits, still holding on under the leaves.

Fall will now always remind me of significant change in my family's country life. This autumn, in an effort to downsize, my wife, Sharon, and I decided to sell the house we had built on 14 acres in the country and move to a town house. It is time to say good-bye to the 40-mile view. The sadness we feel at leaving the place where we raised our daughter, Sara, turned to pride as we considered the hard work and traditional craftsmanship that created that home. We are happy that someone else will enjoy it, and build on what we started. Today, as I mowed the grass for probably the last time before the leaves turn my lawn into a crunchy brown- and rust-colored blanket, I see my neighbor Dick grooming his fields and repairing fences in preparation for winter. This hardworking farmer would agree with my grandparents that we are the trusted stewards of our property. How we pass it on—in what condition—is the measure of our worth as landowners and homeowners.

THINGS TO DO IN OCTOBER

INSIDE
- Test and/or change batteries.
- Reset timers for standard time.
- Inspect windows for condensation.
- Winterize air conditioners.
- Shut off outdoor faucet valves.
- Get your humidifier up and running.
- Update your woodstove.

OUTSIDE
- Put up storm windows and doors and remove screens.
- Check window frames for leaks.
- Disconnect garden hoses and store them inside.

DECK, PORCH, AND PATIO
- Empty dirt from planters.
- Get outdoor furniture ready for winter storage.
- Take care of your hanging plants.

GARAGE AND TOOLSHED
- Get your snowblower up and running.
- Organize your snow-clearing gear.
- Ready yard equipment for storage.

YARD AND LANDSCAPE
- Put up bird feeders.
- Rake or blow leaves.
- Get garden beds ready for winter.
- Prepare new perennial beds.
- Harvest fall crops of hardy root vegetables.
- Protect shrubs with burlap.
- Plant spring-flowering bulbs.
- Have your automatic sprinkler system turned off.

October

O*ctober is what* I call a midway month: a few short weeks that may yield everything from the mild temperatures of Indian summer to a hard frost. This leisurely transitional period gives you a chance to finish yard work and store the tools and gear that you still needed in September; the cold snaps remind you to get out the storm windows and make sure your heating system is ready to go.

*I*NSIDE

■ **Test and/or change batteries in your smoke detectors, automatic garage door remote controls, clocks, and thermostats.** Mechanical thermostats with compound bar sensors do not run on batteries, but digital thermostats with timers and setbacks do. Don't get stuck with a dead battery. Keep extra batteries on hand for your flashlights, too.

■ **Reset timers for standard time.** In addition to the requisite clock setting, you'll want to double-check timers on your furnace, thermostats, heat tapes (on water pipes and gutters), and the heating wires used to melt ice and snow off roof shingles. If you don't have light timers, think about getting some. They're particularly useful for turning on lights inside and out during the months when you leave for work in daylight but return home in the dark. Lights that turn on by timer are an excellent deterrent to intruders when you're away overnight.

■ **Inspect windows for condensation.** Moisture and fog on windows may indicate an air leak. In a regular window, this might result from a loose sash or poorly operating storm window. Air leaks can cause condensation between the glass and the storm window, producing frost. If condensation is collecting between the panes of an insulated thermal window, the seal is leaking. Ever since the oil crisis of the 1970s, an increasing number of homes have been built (or retrofitted) with insulated (thermal) windows to improve energy efficiency. A true thermal window contains two—sometimes three—panes of glass, which are designed to sandwich a pocket of insulating gas between them. The spacer bars

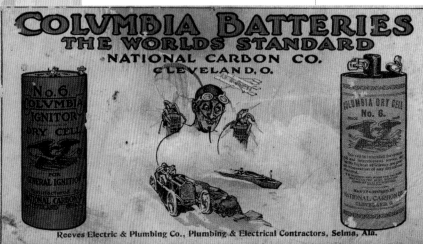

contain an absorbent desiccant, and the whole system is fitted with a tight perimeter seal. A pinhole can break the seal, but in this case condensation may be only a cosmetic problem. The window is probably still insulating (unless there's a really big hole somewhere). If the fog bothers you, or if the window seal is truly compromised, the sash or the insulated glass panels needs replacing. Check with a professional for advice.

TIP Good Window Insulation

Effective storm windows or insulated thermal window sashes are essential. A single glass pane exposed to a room temperature of 70°F and an outdoor temperature of 20°F has an *interior* surface temperature of 32°F! When storms or double- or triple-glazing are used, the interior surface temperature of the glass increases to as much as 52°F.

■ **Winterize air conditioners**. Remove and store window units or fit them with one of the protective covers made for this purpose (available at hardware and home supply stores). Covers are also useful for the exterior condensers of central air-conditioning systems.

TIP Water Valves Most

household fixtures that use water also have individual valves, including one for the toilet, sink, washer, hot-water heater, furnace, refrigerator ice maker, and exterior hose bibs. In certain rooms, such as upstairs bathrooms and the kitchen, a separate valve may operate the "feed" to the whole room or area. Find out where valves are located and familiarize yourself with what they do. Better yet, label them with tags, using a permanent marking pen, so you or members of your family can identify them in case of an emergency.

■ **Shut off outdoor faucet valves.** In cold weather, any water left in exterior pipes and faucets can freeze and expand, breaking the pipes. Most modern systems are fitted with self-draining, frost-free exterior

WARRANTED

Made in Nine Sizes, Square.   Six Sizes with Reservoir and Closet.

=1890=

THE NEW GOLDEN HARVEST,

—WITH—

RESERVOIR AND LOW WARMING CLOSET.

THE **HIGH STANDARD** and POPULARITY of our STOVES in the PAST is **MORE** than MAINTAINED
by our NEW PATTERNS

faucets that don't have to be shut off inside the house with a master valve for the winter. If they are not frost-proof, look for the valve in the basement or crawl space and turn it off by the end of October. If the system is old, the faucets won't be frost-free, so you'll need to go outside and run the faucets to drain them of residual water.

- **Get your humidifier up and running.** If you didn't do a maintenance check last January, do it now. Clean the humidifier thoroughly and dust the outside of it. If you are not allergic to bleach, add a capful of it to the water to ensure that the tank doesn't become a breeding ground for bacteria, unless manufacturer's instructions indicate otherwise. Empty the tank completely before you refill it.

- **Update your woodstove.** One recent statistic notes that some 10 million households in America use wood-burning stoves, but as many as 90 percent do not meet the latest EPA standards, established about a decade ago. If your stove does not have a glass front, it probably predates EPA approval, which is designed to ensure safer, cleaner, and more economical burning. If the woodstove does have EPA approval, a metal tag on the stove should say so.

OUTSIDE

■ **Put up storm windows and doors and remove screens.** If you have separate storms, install them now and remove your screens. Store the screens where they won't get dirty or torn. If you have a triple-track screen/storm-window system, vacuum the screens with a brush attachment. Then slide them up on their track and slide the storm windows down into place. Wash the storms as you would any other window. Check to see that storm windows and doors have a tight seal.

■ **Check window frames for leaks.** Be sure to get up high and check the upper side of the trim above the window, which is a prime spot for water seepage. Gaps there and elsewhere around the window frame can be sealed with polyurethane caulking.

■ **Disconnect garden hoses and store them inside.** Rubber and vinyl hoses will become brittle and crack if left out in freezing temperatures. Extend the life of a hose by taking time to unhook and coil it, and store inside.

THE BIDDING PROCESS

Hiring a professional to paint, build, or make alterations to your home is a serious undertaking. A well-reasoned choice requires a bidding process, in which the candidates submit a detailed statement outlining the fees they would charge to complete the job. Depending on the work to be done, this process begins with a Request for Bid (RFB) from the homeowner and/or architect or engineer. The idea is to be as clear and precise as possible, in writing, about the scope of the work with each candidate. In this way, all the responses (you want a minimum of three) will be based on the same specifications (apples to apples), thus ensuring a balanced comparison. A typical RFB outlines the scope of work, specifies materials needed, the desired start and completion dates, and a request to the bidder to itemize the costs. It will also state when and where the bids are due back in the requester's hands.

The response should also be in writing, covering all the major components of the job. In a building project this might include the excavation, foundation, framing, electric, plumbing, finish work, and landscaping. Although every shingle and door is not enumerated, the bid should list any item that might be considered an option because it could be dropped without a major negative effect on the integrity of the project (a large custom-designed bay window, say). Such itemizing will help you understand the bid and make fair comparisons with the other submissions. It will also highlight the most expensive line items of a project, making it easier to determine what might go to lower the cost and help with cash-flow planning throughout the job.

After reviewing the submissions carefully, meet with each candidate to make sure you understand his or her bid and are confident about what it contains. (You can also leave this step to your architect or engineer.) If all the bids come in over budget, you can still select a contractor and work with him or her to change the plans or specs and downsize the scope of the project. A good professional will suggest ways to save money. It may be possible to phase the project (build the new garage now, say, but finish the room above it next year). In the long run this strategy may actually cost more, because prices can rise in the meantime, and you will have to get the contractor back on the job. But if spreading out expenditures can help you in the short run, that may be a realistic trade-off.

The lowest bid is not always the best: It could actually cost you the most at the end of the project, especially if you aren't communicating well with your contractor. Some contractors bid low and hope to make money on extras, so keep an eye out for this strategy. The hired contractor or painter must stick with the written bid. However, existing but unforeseen conditions (such as hidden pipes buried in the wall) or changes in the specs—at the builder's or homeowner's suggestion or by the architect—can legitimately change the agreed-upon fee.

TIP Insurance Any professional working on your home should have insurance. Ask for proof of that insurance, in the form of an original document mailed directly to you or your architect by the insurance agent. Don't accept a copy, which may not be valid or current. Because good insurance is expensive to carry, a disreputable painter or contractor might try to dupe a customer into believing insurance is in place when it's not.

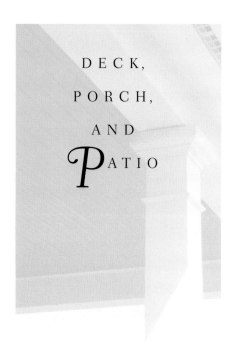

DECK, PORCH, AND $\mathcal{P}$ATIO

- **Empty dirt from planters.**
Flowerpots and planters should be emptied and turned upside down or stored inside. Be sure all dirt is out—if clay pots are in an unheated area, the dirt will freeze and expand and the pots can crack or break.

- **Get outdoor furniture ready for winter storage.** Give porch and deck furniture a final cleaning, dry it thoroughly, and check for any needed repairs. Cover the furniture with a tarpaulin or store it inside a protected area. Cushions make inviting winter nesting spots for mice and other rodents, so pack them in a protected place for the season. Glass tabletops should be brought inside for storage if they are removable; otherwise protect the glass with a piece of plywood cut to size before covering the furniture with a tarp.

- **Take care of your hanging plants.** If you don't plan to winter over your hanging porch and patio plants, you can leave them out until the first cold or frost arrives. But once they are dead, it's important to dispose of the plants immediately. A pot left hanging will just collect snow and ice.

GARAGE AND *T*OOLSHED

■ **Get your snowblower up and running.** Fill it with fresh gas and install new spark plugs. Make sure the oil reservoir is filled to the proper level and change the oil if it is dirty or old. Start the engine and run it for it several minutes, then try the gears. If repairs are in order, get them done now. A small-engine repair shop or lawn mower dealer can service the machine—many will even pick it up and deliver it back.

■ **Organize your snow-clearing gear.** When snow arrives, you want to have shovels, roof rakes, and snowblowers where you can get them—not trapped behind wheelbarrows, rakes, mowers, and all the other gear that you piled into your garage or toolshed at the end of the summer. Take an afternoon to prioritize so your winter gear is handy.

■ **Ready yard equipment for storage.** This includes gas-powered

lawn mowers, edgers, and rotary tillers. Leaving fuel in the tank over the winter can gum up the carburetor of a gasoline tool. If the amount is small, run the motor until the gas is used up, leaving the tank and carburetor empty. Or siphon the gas into a separate container and then run the motor until the tank is empty. To oil the motor, remove the spark plug from the engine and squirt a small amount of automobile oil into the plug hole. Before replacing the spark plug, pull the starter cord several times to disperse the oil. For electric-start equipment, simply turn the key and wait for the engine to turn over for a few seconds to disburse oil over the cylinder. Brush dead cut grass from the blades before storing lawn equipment.

TIP Snow Rakes These tools have telescoping poles (usually 6 to 18 feet long) designed to enable you to scrape snow off your roof as you stand on the ground. This helps prevent damage from heavy loads and the ice dams that form as snow thaws and refreezes near gutters. Take care not to damage shingles or gutters when using a snow rake.

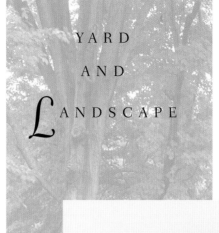

Y A R D

A N D

L A N D S C A P E

■ **Put up bird feeders.** Birds are more likely to come to a porch or deck when you are not using these areas yourself. Put your feeder in view of a window (but not too close or the birds might crash into it) so you'll be able to enjoy the sights. Remember: If you start feeding birds now, you should continue throughout the winter because they will become dependent on the food. Always be sure there is a good supply of food out after a snowstorm.

TIP Discarding Leaves If your town has a pickup service, bag leaves in sturdy leaf bags (unless the town will only pick up unbagged leaves) and leave them at the curb as instructed. Don't burn them without a permit, and consider an alternative even if burning is permitted to avoid sending particulate matter and irritants into the air. If there is no pickup service, chop some leaves up with your lawn mower and add them to the compost pile; bag the rest and take them to the dump. Check first, though. Limited space has led to a ban on leaves and yard trimmings at some landfills. If you have the space on your property, you can dispose of leaves there, but don't pile them in the path of a prevailing wind that will blow them back into the cleared areas.

- **Rake or blow leaves.** The timing for raking leaves is always tricky, and you will probably have to do it more than once. For one thing, trees don't all drop their leaves at the same time. Oak leaves, for example, hold on through the winter. But don't wait to clean up the leaves that have fallen; piled up leaves are more difficult to blow or rake, particularly if it rains or sleets. Clean up leaves once after they start to fall, then a second and possibly third time, three or four weeks later.

- **Get garden beds ready for winter.** After the first hard frost, pull up those dead, slimy annuals that didn't survive. Cut all spent perennials to

the ground (unless they should be cut back in the spring) and try to keep the beds clear of leaves. If you don't, getting them out in the spring

will be that much harder. Chopped leaves can be worked into garden beds as a fall fertilizer.

- **Prepare new perennial beds.** I like to till and prepare new beds in the fall, because the soil turns easier when it's not so wet and compacted. Beds also have a chance to settle over the winter. Using a good shovel, turn over at least six inches of soil. Then add a handful each of well-rotted manure, dampened peat moss, and perhaps wood ash every few feet.

- **Harvest fall crops of hardy root vegetables,** but be vigilant about tossing dead and dying vegetables out of the garden if they are rotting

or slimy. Healthy dead plant material can stay to serve as mulch.

- **Protect shrubs with burlap,** which guards susceptible plants (like rhododendrons) against windburn and prevents branches from breaking under the weight of heavy snow and ice storms. To install burlap snugly around the plant, drive stakes (metal or the wooden tomato variety) around the shrub just at the drip line of the plant. Attach the burlap with wire ties or staples, leaving a gap of a few inches at the bottom for air to circulate and extending it within a few inches of the top of the plant. A burlap windbreak can also be an effective deterrent to deer, as long as there is netting over the top of the shrubs.

- **Plant spring-flowering bulbs.** There's still plenty of time to put in tulips, daffodils, crocuses, grape hyacinths, and narcissus.

- **Have your automatic sprinkler system turned off.** This service should be part of the regular end-of-season maintenance of your sprinkler system. The entire system must be drained of water to prevent freezing, which is usually done by blowing compressed air through the system.

GARDENSENSE

PLANNING FOR FALL COLOR

As early as 285 B.C., Theophrasus commented on the scientific phenomenon of leaves changing color and falling from deciduous trees. Just imagine what the Greek philosopher and natural scientist might have thought if he had lived in New England! The American Northeast is one of the few places in the world where the particular conjunction of light and climatic conditions create spectacular fall color, dependent in part on four broad categories of leaf pigment: chlorophylls, carotenoids, anthocyanins, and tannins. The palette is particularly vibrant some years because of temperature and light: Timing depends largely on the shorter hours of sunlight and cooler (but not freezing) temperatures that follow the summer solstice. Bright reds, for instance, require warm, sunny days followed by night temperatures falling between freezing and 45°F. When photosynthesis is limited by a lack of light near peak season (too much rain or cloudy weather), the leaf colors won't be especially vivid.

HOME *A*LMANAC

One reason New England is such a leaf-peepers' paradise is that a maritime climate moderates temperatures and limits the likelihood of killing frosts in October. Colors usually change when chlorophyll production slows or when leaves start to store tannins or sugars as temperatures cool. Even evergreens display fall colors, but we don't notice them, because evergreens don't drop all their needles or leaves at once; the change is gradual. As the inner layer is turning yellow or brown, new green needles are growing on the ends of branches.

Though I don't reside in New England, I have the great good fortune to live where the maple is still king. I pity anyone who can't experience the flaming foliage of this tree in the fall. Sugar maples, which range south to the Carolinas and west to Kansas, are justifiably famous for their brilliant oranges, yellows, and reds—and for their sap. (A single tree can yield up to 60 gallons.) New England settlers learned from Native Americans how to boil the running sap in early spring to make maple sugar and syrup. The red maple, which grows south to Florida and west to Texas—the greatest north-south distribution of any tree species on the Atlantic Seaboard—is another standard-bearer of color.

Fall may not always be the right time for planting shrubs and trees for autumn hues, but it's certainly the time of year to note whatever plants in your region produce colors you might consider for the future. The yellow poplar, the sassafras tree, the white ash (leaves turn purple or yellow), the pecan and black walnut (yellow), the scarlet oak, the black tupelo, and the birch are just a few of the tree types whose leaves yield interesting fall colors—some more subtle than others. Witch hazels, summersweets, Japanese maples, burning bush, and oak-leaf hydrangea are among the shrubs and ornamental trees to consider. You might also notice which plants produce berries at this time of year. One of my favorites is an old native standby, the staghorn sumac, whose glossy leaves and showy fruit clusters make it a popular ornamental; it can be invasive, however, so try to keep the plant's suckers under control.

My advice is to get a good field guide and take a walk, identifying any species you don't already know. Visit a botanical garden or a garden center to determine which shrubs and trees you like. Even plants that are still balled-and-burlapped change color before dropping leaves. Finally, don't forget to note the texture and color of the bark of various woody plants, the shape of the tree or shrub, and the way the bark looks when wet. There is nothing quite like the sight of a sugar maple on a rainy day, its trunk and branches deep black against a backdrop of flaming red and orange foliage.

INSIDE

- Take winter clothes and linens out of storage.
- Check vents.
- Set and/or adjust heat and hot-water thermostats for energy efficiency.
- Prevent the overload of electrical circuits.

OUTSIDE

- Clean gutters and downspouts.
- Clear roof valleys of fallen leaves.
- Check your fuel tank for problems.
- Make sure your fuel tank is clear of water.
- Examine foundations for cracks.

DECK, PORCH, AND PATIO

- Inspect supports, railings, and stairs.
- Make sure all light fixtures are operating.

GARAGE AND TOOLSHED

- Put away motorized lawn and landscape equipment.
- Store your garden tools.
- Provide good drainage around garage entrances.

YARD AND LANDSCAPE

- Make sure culverts and drainage ditches aren't clogged.
- Remove the last fallen leaves.
- Apply winter mulch.
- Clear frequently used areas.
- Protect your lawn and garden beds with driveway markers.
- Make one final cut with your lawn mower.

November

According to the ancient Roman calendar, which begins in March, November is the ninth month of the year. Even as number 11, it still comes too early for me. Though November brings shorter days, I always look forward to the first real snowfall. And of course there's always Thanksgiving to enjoy. If you don't get as much done this month as you think you should, don't worry—you can make up for it after the holidays.

*I*NSIDE

- **Take winter clothes and linens out of storage.** You may want to dry clean anything you packed in mothballs to remove the camphor odor. Toss out herbal moth repellents; they'll lose their potency, and you'll want to use fresh herbs when you repack next spring.

- **Check vents**. Close any vents in unheated basement areas, but keep attic vents open. For extra insulation, cover them on the inside with a piece of inexpensive foam board cut to fit. Make sure that any exhaust fans in your kitchen and bathrooms are

clean; if they have filters, replace them now. To avoid clogs, cracks, and breaks in the winter, check that vents to the outdoors from gas hot-water heaters are in good shape. Replace rusted or damaged venting pipes from gas water heaters and your dryer. If you have vents in your eaves, make sure these are clean and clear of wasps' nests and weren't painted over when you had your house painted.

- **Set and/or adjust heat and hot-water thermostats for energy efficiency.** If you have multiple thermostats in your home for different zones, set temperatures for the way you use the rooms: bedrooms cooler, baths and sitting areas warmer. Thermostats in rooms that are seldom used during cold weather can be lowered for the whole season.

- **Prevent the overload of electrical circuits.** Plugging in a space heater is a good way to overburden an outlet or circuit. Make sure wires aren't hot and regard dimming lights as a warning that you are overloading your home's electrical capacities. Blowing a fuse or tripping a breaker is a sure sign. Make certain that electrical cords are not covered by rugs or blocked by heavy curtains; the cords can cause a fire if they overheat, which sometimes happens before a fuse blows.

TIP Carbon Monoxide Poisoning The potentially fatal effects of carbon monoxide are a particular risk in the winter, when storm windows, closed doors, extra weather-stripping, and other cold-weather measures create a "tight" house. Carbon monoxide is an invisible, odorless predator that can leak into your home from malfunctioning gas furnaces and stoves, water heaters, generators, improperly vented fireplaces, and the exhaust from running cars. Headache, grogginess, and scratchy throat are all symptoms of carbon monoxide poisoning. The best defense is a carbon monoxide detector designed to sound an alarm and indicate possible problems on a digital display. Because carbon monoxide is heavier than air, the detectors should be placed close to the floor. A plug-in model that can go right into a wall outlet, usually a foot or so off the floor, is a good idea.

OUTSIDE

■ **Clean gutters and downspouts.** At some point during November, most of the leaves will have fallen, though a healthy oak may keep its leaves until spring. After leaves have dropped, clean out your gutters and make sure the downspouts aren't blocked. Clogged gutters are one of the causes of ice dams (see "Look for Ice Dams and Water Leaks," January). You may want to invest in a gutter scoop specifically designed for the job.

■ **Clear roof valleys of fallen leaves.** The line where two slanted roof sections join in a V, known as a *valley*, can be a trouble spot when dead leaves and pine needles collect there, preventing proper drainage into the gutters. The upside-down V, known as a *cricket*, behind the chimney should also be cleared. You may need to get up on the roof with a ladder and clear leaves and debris with a broom or small rake.

■ **Check your fuel tank for problems.** Make sure external fuel lines are in good shape. Insulate any exposed lines (these can be buried or wrapped in waterproof tape). If you have an in-ground oil tank, mark the fuel pipe with a driveway marker so your oil company can find it in the snow. Ask if your oil supplier uses an anticondensation agent. The general wisdom is that it should be added to the oil tank every time you refill to prevent interior rusting and

decay. The last thing you want is a hole in your oil tank.

Are in-ground oil tanks still legal? Yes, they are usually "grandfathered" in from previous permits. If an in-ground tank is leaking, however, you are responsible for the cleanup. Your oil company can test the tank with a simple pressure test, which may require a bit of digging. If there is a problem, you should bring up the tank and have it changed to a double-walled or fiberglass model or switch to an indoor tank. If you ever want to sell your house, an in-ground tank must be tested—another reason to solve problems now.

- **Make sure your fuel tank is clear of water**. Because it is heavier than oil, water will sink to the bottom of a tank, where it can cause rust. An older tank, especially an in-ground one, may have a good amount of water in it. Water may get in through the breather pipe (which lets air in and out when the tank is being filled or emptied) or from condensation. Your service company can check for water and draw it out if necessary.

- **Examine foundations for cracks**. Snow and water in cracks can cause frost damage. Repair as necessary.

DESIGNBOOK

ANATOMY OF A COLUMN

Columns are a fundamental element in classical design—and one of the most basic components in architecture—because they serve as primary load-bearing supports. In the term *post-and-beam*, the *post* is the vertical column, and the *beam* is the horizontal element it carries. In a post-and-beam barn or house, the columns are typically just squared posts, often hand-hewn and left exposed to reveal the texture of the timbers.

In classical architecture, however, a column has very distinct design features and mathematical proportions. Both were strictly prescribed by the ancient Greeks and Romans, who developed the prototypical classical orders (Doric, Ionic, and Corinthian) to ensure harmony of design. In most orders, the column consists of a round (often fluted) stone *shaft*, set atop a *base* and crowned by a *capital*. It's easy to identify a particular order by the design of the capital; most people, for instance, are familiar with the ornate *acanthus leaves* that distinguish the Corinthian order or the scrolled *volutes* of the Ionic capital. In a classical building, the column supports the *entablature*, which consists of *architrave*, *frieze*, and the topmost finishing element, the *cornice*.

The classical architecture of ancient Rome, revived during the Italian Renaissance, was celebrated in a number of beautifully illustrated books published in England during the 17th and 18th centuries. Archeological excavations in Rome and Greece during the 1700s generated enormous interest throughout Britain, France, and America. Design specifications for the classical columns and entablatures used in Georgian, Federal, and Greek Revival architecture from the early 1700s to the mid-1800s were widely published in the pocket guides and pattern books that early American architects and builders used. Though some were followed scrupulously and others translated freely in the vernacular, the basic elements and terms have endured as part of a familiar architectural vocabulary with roots dating back thousands of years.

CHOOSING PAINT COLORS

Despite what decorating magazines may say, choosing paint colors is largely a matter of common sense. Most people don't need someone to tell them that the color they select for their living room walls shouldn't clash with the sofa they already own. And how many people ever consult a color wheel or get inspiration for decorating their master bedroom from medieval tapestries at a museum?

That said, a few pieces of advice concerning paint are worth offering. One is to start with paint chips. Those stacks of cards striped with paint colors in shades of the same family (a range of yellows, say) that you see in display racks at paint and hardware stores are yours for the taking. Choose a bunch in the colors you are considering, take them home, and use

them. Inside, check the color chips (next to fabrics and rugs) in the rooms you plan to paint under different lighting conditions. The same hue can look surprisingly different under incandescent light and natural sunlight. Use the same logic outdoors: Look at

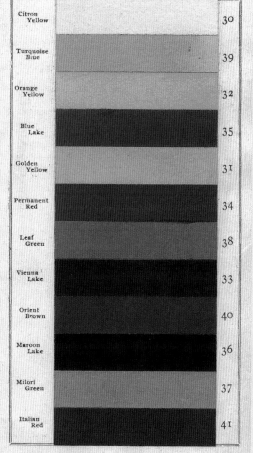

Courtesy Benjamin Moore & Co.

...MURESCO COLORS...

Are intended for use where darker shades than our Muresco Tints are desired; also for tinting colors in connection with our Tinting White Muresco. They are adapted to all kinds of wall and ceiling decorating, fresco painting, plain tinting, etc., and will be found much more satisfactory and economical than the use of dry or distemper colors, as well as a great improvement over any other line of dry sized colors heretofore offered to the trade. Many colors are not adapted to water color work, and it is impossible to get good results from their use, but Muresco colors are made expressly for this purpose and never fail to give perfect satisfaction. They are ground fine, work easy, cover perfectly, flow on smoothly and dry flat, without clouds, brush marks or flashing, making a clear, soft and velvet-like surface. By combining these colors together an endless variety of handsome shades are produced. Ask for our Decorators' book showing a large line of combination colors.

For light shades see card showing Muresco Tints.

PRICE LIST.

	1 lb. Packages	5 lb. Packages	50 or 100 lb. Drums
Nos. 31, 40.......Per lb.	24c.	22c.	20c
" 30, 32, 35, 41.... " "	32c.	30c.	28c
" 37, 38............ " "	42c.	40c.	38c
" 36, 39............ " "	44c.	42c.	40c
" 33, 34............ " "	46c.	44c.	42c

Packages are put up in 50 or 100 lb. cases, assorted if desired.

MANUFACTURED ONLY BY

BENJAMIN MOORE & CO.

NEW YORK AND CHICAGO

Color	No.
Citron Yellow	30
Turquoise Blue	39
Orange Yellow	32
Blue Lake	35
Golden Yellow	31
Permanent Red	34
Leaf Green	38
Vienna Lake	33
Orient Brown	40
Maroon Lake	36
Milori Green	37
Italian Red	41

prospective colors at various times of day and compare colors for siding and trim under different conditions.

Exterior Paint: In choosing exterior colors, start with something you like. Don't forget to check with town officials to see if there are restrictions on paint colors in your neighborhood—a likelihood if your house is in a historic district. Note how other houses are painted, and also consider how the color of your house may look next to that of a neighboring home.

A traditional approach in exterior house painting is to opt for a neutral color (white, off-white, gray, light green, or brown) with a brighter or contrasting shade of trim, but generalizing is almost pointless. These guidelines may be useless, for example, if you are replicating a multihued Victorian paint scheme. Conventional wisdom maintains that darker colors fade more easily than lighter shades, but the truth is that we probably just notice the difference more readily. At some point, any paint exposed to the elements will fade.

Shingles can be left untreated to weather on their own, but they take years to achieve a uniform "weathered" look, except when exposed to salt air—then they go gray fairly quickly and become mottled or blotchy. For a more uniform look, you can seal them, but sealed shingles need cleaning and resealing every few years.

Interior Paint: House paint comes in two basic types: alkyd (oil-based) and latex (water-based). The former is more durable, but requires paint thinner or turpentine for cleanup, while the latter is easier to use because you can wash equipment and spills with water. (Some latex paints, however, are subject to "blocking," which means that they stay tacky even after the paint has dried—not a good thing for bookshelves or furniture.)

Paint also comes in different finishes. (Interior paints are available in flat, eggshell, satin, semigloss, and gloss.) The choice is dictated partly by the look you want (sheen or no sheen) and the practicality of using a finish in a particular place. For interiors, a flat or eggshell finish is generally recommended for walls because it has a soft, neutral surface that doesn't reflect. Semigloss, on the other hand, is the favored choice for interior trim (doors, window frames, baseboards, cornices, and moldings) because it can take some real scrubbing, and these areas tend to get grimy. Flat is good for ceilings.

The staff of a reputable paint or decorating store can recommend the right paint for any surface—from radiators to ceilings to exterior trim to porch floors—and can also suggest the best brushes and rollers to use, if you're doing the painting.

One final recommendation: Buy the best paint your budget can handle. A high-quality paint is worth the investment because it will ensure easier brushing or rolling, and will minimize brush marks and misting (if you use a roller), blocking, and fading. When in doubt, consult a professional.

WHY HIRE AN ARCHITECT OR ENGINEER?

When cold weather rolls around, I always find myself thinking about new building projects. If you're considering one, sooner or later you'll have to decide whether you want or need an architect or engineer. Many major remodeling projects call for one or both because most municipalities require stamped plans by an engineer or architect to issue a building permit. If the job is large or complex, you will need to supply architectural plans to get an accurate bid on the building costs, anyway.

If you need plans and aren't sure what you can do or even what you want, I strongly recommend that you engage a professional architect or engineer to design the project and guide you through the building process. Many contractors will supply plans or design services as well. Some have in-house architects with the credentials to stamp the plans or are aligned with professionals qualified to do so. (Such contracting firms are often known as design-build firms.)

In terms of design know-how, certain jobs fall well within the skills of a good, experienced contractor: a remodeling job like a new bath or kitchen (replacing fixtures and tiles, say), replacing siding or a roof, designing a garage, or matching something that already exists.

The first thing to know, however, is that contractors want to be paid for design services, either by charging up front (if they are part of a competitive bidding process; see "The Bidding Process," October) or by rolling the cost into their total fee. They rarely leave you the plans unless you have paid for them or signed a contract to do the work with them.

Don't sign up a contractor you haven't worked with previously as a design supervisor. For one thing, learning about the construction process is enough to deal with. A less-than-honorable contractor can tailor the design plans he or she provides to pad his or her own pockets or make the scope of work more manageable—you may not know enough to recognize this.

If you know and trust your contractor, however, giving him or her the responsibility of overseeing the design process can be a wise decision. The contractor can be on your side throughout the process, including hiring and supervising the architect or engineer for you. If your relationship is good, you won't be left out of the loop. Clients who know me well often ask me to hire an architect and develop a budget incorporating that expense. The advantage of this strategy is that contractor and architect are developing the plan in sync, and both are familiar with all the details. The budget is more accurate because extras and surprises are kept to a minimum. *Remember: Choose this approach only if you know and trust your contractor.*

A good architect can answer questions, clarify the design items for the bidders, and rework plans to accommodate your budget if necessary. Beware of any architect (or contractor, for that matter) who tries to control the budget by vetoing suggestions for reasonable "cost engineering" (as it is called in the trade) to reduce expenses. If you do change the scope of the work, let the architect redraw or offer suggestions. Try to resist the temptation to begin putting back into the plan everything that you just took out.

DECK, PORCH, AND *P*ATIO

- **Inspect supports, railings, and stairs.** Are they in good repair? A flimsy handrail, for example, might give way when someone slipping on ice or snow grabs it suddenly. Make sure that the footings under the support posts are in good shape and have not shifted or heaved because of water, settling, or frost.

- **Make sure all light fixtures are operating.** Don't let lightbulbs near porches and patios burn out. You don't want to signal would-be burglars that some areas of your home aren't being used or watched.

GARAGE
AND
*T*OOLSHED

- **Put away motorized lawn and landscape equipment.** When you have finished the last of your outdoor chores, run the motor of your tractor or mower to empty the gas tank for storage. Follow the manufacturer's directions for storing it during the off-season. Drain the fuel from all gas-operated equipment, such as leaf blowers and chain saws.

- **Store your garden tools.** Clean your trowels, claws, and other hand tools and apply a light coat of vegetable oil to prevent rust.

- **Provide good drainage around garage entrances.** Regrading to make the ground level, or slope away from the entrance, will prevent ice and water buildup during storms. Otherwise, clear ice and snow away to prevent creating a dam and sending water in the wrong direction.

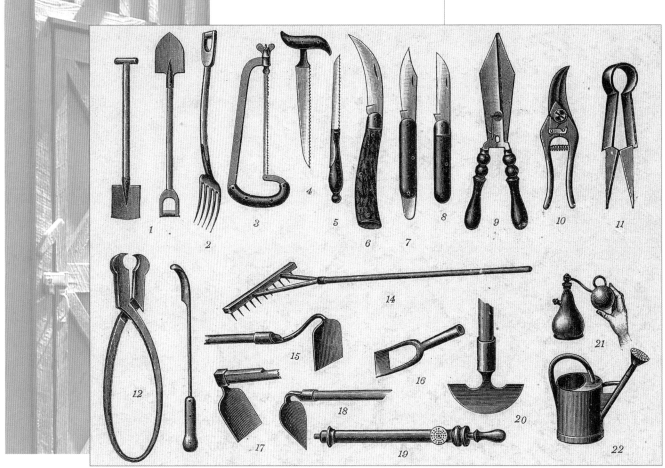

YARD AND LANDSCAPE

- **Make sure culverts and drainage ditches aren't clogged.** Clogs can cause flooding and/or dangerous ice sheeting over your drive. Clear culverts of fallen leaves and twigs.

- **Remove the last fallen leaves.** Even if you started leaf cleanup in October, you'll probably need a final raking. A leaf collection bag attached to your lawn mower will make the job easier.

- **Apply winter mulch.** In areas where snow cover is not deep enough to give plants any real insulation, winter mulches can help mitigate damage from frost heaves and temperature fluctuations. Wait until after the ground freezes. If you mulch prematurely, small animals that might otherwise go elsewhere may nest in the warm covering; mulching before a freeze can also promote mildew.

    Some perennials, like peonies and irises, do better without winter mulch.

- **Clear frequently used areas around your house, such as pathways and stoops,** to make shoveling snow easier. This is another argument for putting away large flowerpots. Make sure there is good access to your woodpile, gas and oil tanks, and garbage cans.

- **Protect your lawn and garden beds with driveway markers.** A well-marked driveway helps keep the snowplow operator from straying onto your lawn. You can buy metal markers topped with red reflectors. If you don't like the look, try tomato stakes or erect a snow fence. Tell your plow operator where excess snow should be piled. You want to avoid dumping a mountain of plowed snow on your lawn, especially if your driveway is paved with loose stone. Leaving enough room for cars to turn and park safely is equally important.

- **Make one final cut with your lawn mower.** Trim grass height to two inches; otherwise the ends will die, creating a thatch that is detrimental to spring growth.

INSIDE

- Prevent water pipes from freezing.
- Look for condensation on window glass.
- Assess extra insulation needs.
- Maintain your humidifier.
- Ventilate your attic.
- Regulate water temperature to conserve energy.

OUTSIDE

- Watch for ice dams.
- Make sure outside hose bibs are shut off and drained.
- Survey security needs.
- Install halogen bulbs in outdoor fixtures.
- Check for winter-damage trouble spots.
- Prevent locks from freezing.

DECK, PORCH, AND PATIO

- Keep porches, decks, and patios clear of snow.
- Maintain storage bins.
- Create winter planters and window boxes.

GARAGE AND TOOLSHED

- Make sure snow equipment is ready for action.
- Keep vehicles fueled and in good repair.
- Don't let ice and snow pile up around garage doors.
- Maintain garage door tracks.

YARD AND LANDSCAPE

- Do a final survey of your gardens.
- Feed the birds.

December

*C*ome December, I'm *ready* for winter to roll around. As far as I'm concerned, a really good coating of snow hides a multitude of sins in the yard. This early in the season, winter chores like shoveling the front walk still seem more a pleasure than a duty. And I look forward to cold days, when I can justify puttering around the house or holing up in my workshop. Let it snow, let it snow, let it snow.

*I*NSIDE

■ **Prevent water pipes from freezing.**
In most regions, December is usually the first month when you are likely to encounter perilous deep freezes. If a large temperature drop is forecast—and if your kitchen and bathroom sink pipes freeze in cold weather—leave the cabinet doors under the sink open overnight. Another useful practice is to let faucets drip very gently so water doesn't freeze in the pipes. Insulate any pipes that may freeze, especially those in an uninsulated attic.

TIP Holiday Evergreen Care To keep evergreen boughs fresh longer, soak the cut ends for 24 hours before arranging. Unless greens have just been cut, make a fresh slash on the ends and put them in a solution of half a cup of brown sugar to a gallon of water. If you have a live tree, check the water every day and replenish as necessary; a fresh tree can drink a quart or more of water daily. When the water use slows or stops, the tree is drying out. Don't place a cut tree near any heat source, such as a fireplace, woodstove, television, radiator, or hot-air duct.

- **Look for condensation on window glass.** Moisture indicates the need to increase ventilation around the glass, which may be as simple as loosening curtains or blinds or lowering the humidifier setting. You may need to add storm windows if you don't have them or use plastic storms on the inside.

- **Assess extra insulation needs.** Among the trouble spots are floors above unheated crawl spaces and basements and walls that separate living areas from those that are unheated (such as a garage). Do these surfaces seem cold to the touch? The easiest insulation to install in these situations is the fiberglass type that comes in blanket or batt form and is sized in varying widths to fit between floor joists, wall studs, and ceiling rafters. Both come without backing (to supplement existing insulation) and backed (often with foil, to be used facing the heated part of the house) to provide a vapor barrier. A vapor barrier will protect against the dampness that results in winter when moisture is drawn through walls, ceilings, and floors toward the drier air outside the house. Moisture migration occurs as the humidity levels inside and out try to reach a natural equilibrium. On the way out, the moisture reaches the dew point, which is the temperature at which water vapor condenses on a surface. Wet insulation is not good: The condensation becomes a heat conductor, transferring warmth out and inhibiting the insulation's ability to trap air in its pockets. Always install the vapor barrier on the warm side of the surface so that moisture is stopped before it moves through and reaches the dew point. Condensation in a wall or on the backside of exterior siding can cause rotting or peeling paint.

TIP Mind Your R's and U's Find out about R-values before you buy insulation materials. The R-value is a number that indicates the resistance of an insulation material to winter heat loss or summer heat gain. Sources for information about R-value ratings include the Department of Energy, the National Institute of Standards and Technology, the U.S. Department of Commerce, and insulation manufacturers. Products like doors and windows may also be marked with a U-factor, which is a measure of the flow of heat that may be lost. The lower the U-factor and the higher the R-factor, the better.

- **Maintain your humidifier.** These appliances should be cleaned regularly during the heating season; otherwise, bacteria and the spores from fungi that grow in dirty water tanks mist out into your home along with the moisture you want. A film of fine white dust that collects on your furniture is likely the result of mineral deposits being dispersed from the humidifier tank. To avoid problems, use distilled or demineralized water rather than tap water. The water in portable humidifiers should be changed at least every third day. (If you have a console unit, change the water as often as the manufacturer suggests.) Clean scum or mineral deposits in the tank with a sponge or brush. If demineralization cartridges, filters, or cassettes are recommended for use with your humidifier, be sure you have some extras on hand.

TIP Breathing Lessons You shouldn't pack insulation too densely. Because insulation works by trapping air pockets, packing it too tightly forces the air out. Insulation should fill the crack or cavity being insulated neatly and snugly, but not so tightly that there is no room for it to breathe.

■ **Ventilate your attic.** Attic fans can be as helpful in cold weather as in the summer. If you don't have attic vents, use your fan to draw out excess moisture and keep the space cool. If you do have vents, make sure they are clear and operating. I recommend running an electric fan (in the gable or roof, to vent the attic only). The fan should be on a timer, or on a humidistat or thermostat set to turn it off when the moisture or temperature is at the desired level. If you pull out too much air in winter, you can draw heat out of the house.

■ **Regulate water temperature to conserve energy.** To prevent scalds, set the heater's thermostat no higher than 120°F. To determine the water temperature, draw water from the bottom faucet and test it with a thermometer. The best way to save on hot water is to use a lot less of it (shorter showers and less-than-full tubs). Lowering the temperature of hot water doesn't necessarily save energy because you may wind up putting more hot water into the tub to get the temperature as hot as you are used to. Consider a shower: It's better for your skin anyway. Hot-water heaters and tanks can be insulated for better energy efficiency—and electric ones should always be insulated.

GET SMART

10 TIPS FOR SAVING ENERGY IN COLD WEATHER

1. When you use your fireplace, close the doors and heating ducts in the room and open a window near the fireplace about half an inch. This provides the air needed for the fire to burn while reducing the amount of heated air drawn from the rest of the house.

2. If you have an open masonry fireplace, consider installing a glass screen, convective grate, a combination convective grate/screen, or a radiant grate or fireplace insert. Any of these devices can reduce the amount of warm air lost up a chimney.

3. When the heat is on, lower the thermostat to about 65°F during the day and 60°F at night.

4. Keep windows near your thermostat tightly sealed.

5. Don't let cold air seep into your home through the attic door. Make sure it is well insulated and weather-stripped; otherwise, you will be wasting fuel to heat that cool air.

6. Do as much household cleaning as possible with cold water.

7. Insulate your hot-water storage tank and piping.

8. Use cold water to run the food disposer to save energy.

9. Let dishes air dry in the dishwasher. If you don't have an automatic air-dry control, turn off the machine after the final rinse. Then prop the door open with a wooden spoon to hasten the drying.

10. If you don't have an automatic defroster, defrost your refrigerator regularly. Frost buildup increases the amount of energy needed to keep the motor running.

FORCING BULBS

The term *forcing* seems a little heavy-handed for the very benign and satisfying act of coaxing bulb flowers to bloom indoors in winter. *Tricking* is more like it, because you're really manipulating temperatures and growing conditions to make the bulb think it's time to flower. This technique works particularly well with spring-blooming bulbs like narcissus, hyacinths, and tulips, because these plants bloom naturally after a period of dormancy that you can simulate quite easily indoors. Normally, the bulb is planted outdoors in the fall and has the benefit of cold temperatures throughout the winter dormancy period. It flowers in spring when the air and ground temperatures rise. To force a bulb indoors, you essentially create the same kind of conditions, starting with specially prechilled bulbs (hyacinths are sometimes sold this way) or bulbs you chill in the refrigerator. Paperwhite narcissus are among the easiest bulbs to force, because they bloom pretty dependably after a few weeks of cold storage (check with a garden center about the cold requirements of different bulb plants).

If you want potted plants, you should plant the bulbs in a special bulb medium (available at garden centers) or in a porous, fast-draining potting mix. Plant a few bulbs pointed side up to a pot, leaving room for the roots to spread, and store the pot in a cool, dark location where the temperature is between freezing and 40°F. Keep the bulbs stored for the recommended dormancy period, moistening the soil from time to time. If you are not potting the bulbs, then simply put them in a paper bag and store them in your refrigerator for the dormancy period.

When you are ready for the bulbs to flower (blooming time is usually two to three weeks), take the pots or bulbs out of cold storage. If you haven't potted the bulbs, you can try clustering them, pointed end up, in a shallow tray of plant pebbles filled with water. The problem is that long-stemmed flowers like narcissus tend to topple, so you may need to tie up your cluster with string once the stems have shot up. The alternative is to place bulbs, one each, in wineglasses (with water); the glass will provide enough support when the stem shoots up. And a group of these make a dramatic arrangement on a mantel or windowsill. You can buy bulb glasses for the same purpose, but why bother, when wineglasses work so well?

Plants will sprout when you place the bulbs (in trays, glasses, or pots) in a cool spot—about 60°F—for a week or so. When they begin sprouting, put them in full sunlight so they can flower. Though forced bulbs won't flower twice indoors this way, you can save the bulbs and plant them outside the following fall.

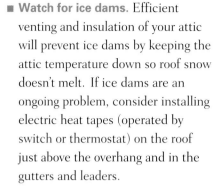

OUTSIDE

■ **Watch for ice dams.** Efficient venting and insulation of your attic will prevent ice dams by keeping the attic temperature down so roof snow doesn't melt. If ice dams are an ongoing problem, consider installing electric heat tapes (operated by switch or thermostat) on the roof just above the overhang and in the gutters and leaders.

■ **Make sure outside hose bibs are shut off and drained.** This isn't necessary if you have frost-proof fittings, but it's obligatory otherwise.

■ **Survey the exterior of your house to make sure security remains good.** Despite the supposed good

cheer of the season, the rate of break-ins and burglaries rises during the holidays. Your house is more likely to be targeted when you are out at a party or away on vacation. Therefore, it's more important than ever to be sure that all of your outdoor light sensors are working. Don't let newspapers and mail pile up, and be sure plowing and shoveling are done promptly when you are away.

■ **Install halogen bulbs in outdoor fixtures.** If you didn't do this last winter, do it now. Halogen bulbs are better suited for exterior fixtures than indoor ones because they generate so much heat—in fact, when used inside you should be careful to keep them away from lampshades and curtains. They are also more energy efficient than the incandescent bulbs typically used inside.

■ **Check for winter-damage trouble spots**. Examine windowsills and wood trim for signs of water seepage, cracking, and damage from rusting nails. Spot-check the roof eaves for rot and keep checking the foundation for leaks.

■ **Prevent locks from freezing.** Locks should be kept lubricated and dry to prevent rust, freeze-ups, and excess wear on both lock and key. The best lubricant is silicone, which provides a good coating for the lock parts and repels water. A really cold, damp climate calls for graphite lubrication. Avoid oil, which can gum up the works and attract grime. Ask your local locksmith for the best type of lubricant for your climate and the type of locks you have.

THE BOTTOM LINE

HOME INSURANCE

The essential rule of thumb for insurance is to buy as much as you can reasonably afford. Periodically (once a year or no longer than two years), ask your agent for advice about additional (or less) coverage, as needed. At the least, consult your agent every time you make a change, increase your liability risk—by installing a swimming pool, for example—or think you may have increased exposure to a potential problem.

Basic homeowner's coverage should include fire insurance and some liability. In general, a homeowner's policy will cover fire and liability as a package, as well as possibilities you might never suspect, like someone stealing a camera from your car. Always check with your agent to be sure you understand your coverage and report any loss or problem right away—you may be covered without even realizing it.

Fire insurance covers damage and may also finance additional costs of living while your home is repaired or rebuilt, such as rent for temporary quarters. Typically, the contents of a house are insured at an additional value up to 50 percent of the policy amount. (If you have $200,000 worth of fire insurance, the contents would be valued up to another $100,000.) Check with your agent, because state laws may dictate mandatory amounts in a certain jurisdiction. Some policies won't pay the entire cost of the damage if the face value of the policy was not at least 80 percent of the market or replacement value, not counting the land. A few of these contingencies have been outlawed, but you get the idea—consult your agent and don't be afraid to call often, especially at renewal time. Your agent won't mind, particularly if it gives him or her a chance to sell you more. Purchase more coverage only if you need to: A good agent will not sell you more than you need or can afford.

Liability insurance protects you against a lawsuit for damages and injuries to others on your property, and sometimes off your property—as when your lawn mower shoots a stone into a neighbor's window. This insurance is important for obvious reasons, but most people don't realize that an insurance company's first obligation is to defend you in court. This feature means that you don't have to pay a lawyer to represent you when confronted with a legal action. And if there is a judgment against you, the company must pay up to the amount for which you are covered. You can purchase what is known as an umbrella policy, which extends your liability coverage in units of $1 million, usually at the cost of a relatively small premium (a couple of hundred dollars) over and above your other premiums. If you can afford it, or if you have a lot to lose, you should have this extra coverage. It can also extend to other matters, like auto accidents.

Some policies dictate that you must list separately any valuables worth more than a certain amount. Unless listed and covered separately, for example, a ring worth $3,000 may be covered only up to $200 as a general jewelry item. Always ask your agent about jewelry, antiques, paintings, and collectibles.

You may need other special insurance, such as protection against flood or storm damage or natural disasters. In some places this type of coverage is mandated, either by law or by the mortgage holder. Check with the municipality, your lawyer, your real estate agent, or your insurance agent.

DECK,
PORCH,
AND
*P*ATIO

■ **Keep porches, decks, and patios clear of snow** even if you aren't using them. This is a good security measure, *especially* if you aren't using these areas. Letting snow pile up on a porch near an unused back door, for example, can signal that this area is unused and unwatched—and a good place for a burglar to work on the lock. Snow may also block an entrance you need access to in an emergency.

■ **Maintain storage bins.** Outdoor storage areas should be tightly sealed for the winter, which may mean temporarily nailing or screwing lids and doors shut. Securing these areas is also a good way to keep them from becoming attractive nesting areas for squirrels, mice, and other winter rodents.

■ **Create winter planters and window boxes.** Use winter greens, dried leaves, twigs, pinecones, and berries to design waterless arrangements—this idea is particularly good for built-in planters that you can't put away anyway. Protected under a porch roof or in a windless corner of a deck, such arrangements can last for several months and will cheer you up on a gray winter day.

GARAGE AND *T*OOLSHED

- **Make sure snow equipment is ready for action.** The first December snowstorm can catch you unaware. Before you start your snowblower, check the engine oil level and the adjustment of the clutch and chute position. Be sure the tires are properly inflated. If you have an electric snowblower, check the condition of the power cord. Be sure you know how to stop the machine and turn the engine off quickly. You may want to keep a can of starting fluid handy in case of bitter cold weather.

- **Keep vehicles fueled and in good repair.** This is important if severe weather is forecast. Store a winter emergency kit containing a flashlight, blanket, bottled water, and first-aid kit in each car.

- **Don't let ice and snow pile up around garage doors.** After each plowing, make sure that your garage is accessible and cars can get out easily. In the event of a power outage during a storm, you may decide to leave; you don't need the extra aggravation of having to shovel your way out.

- **Maintain garage door tracks.** Icy conditions can be hard on your garage doors.

You may need to lubricate springs and hinges with a spray silicone or light oil. It's important to check rollers, springs, hinges, and tracks periodically to make sure that they are clean, lubricated, and in good operating condition. Electrical openers need the same inspections. Check your manual. If you don't have a manual, ask an overhead door supplier for one or for some generic guidelines.

TIP Automatic Door Safety If your electricity is out and your car is in, you could be stuck in an emergency. Learn how to operate automatic garage doors manually in the event of a power outage. Your doors should also have an automatic stop-and-reverse feature, which is usually controlled by an electronic eye and/or a pressure switch. If the door senses pressure or motion, as though something (or someone) is caught under it, it will stop and reverse direction. All automatic doors installed after January 1, 1993, are required to have this safety device. If you are unsure whether yours is properly equipped, call an overhead door company.

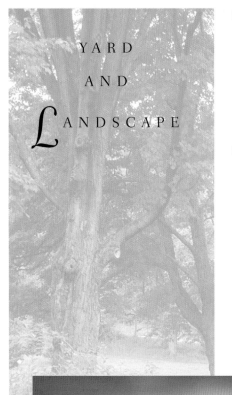

Y A R D

A N D

$\mathcal{L}$ A N D S C A P E

■ **Do a final survey of your gardens.** Have you missed any markers, small statues, or ornaments that should be stored in a protected area for the season? Statues and planters made of plaster or clay can crack or break in repeated freeze-thawing cycles.

■ **Feed the birds.** Even if you have a feeder on your deck or porch, consider one or two for the yard. Different types of seeds attract different types of birds: chickadees, cardinals, jays, and sparrows, for example, are among the varieties that relish black oil sunflower seeds (preferable to striped sunflower seeds); woodpeckers adore suet, also a favorite of chickadees, titmice, and nuthatches. Birds can be quite choosy and are apt to look down their beaks at buckwheat, cracked corn, and German millet, preferring red or white proso millet and the sunflower seeds. So avoid using cheap seed mixes that use lots of filler because you'll likely find most of it relegated to an unappreciated heap under the feeder.

TIP Preparing for a Live Christmas Tree If you are one of the many people experimenting with buying a live tree with balled roots, you should dig a hole for it before there is a sustained freeze— early December should still be fine in most planting zones. Put the dirt in a wheelbarrow and store it temporarily in your garage or potting shed to keep it from freezing; you can wheel it right back to the hole when you plant. In cold climates, a tree with balled roots should be kept indoors no longer than a week, or it will have trouble acclimating to the conditions outside. This may seem a lot of effort for only a week's worth of Christmas tree, but it's a great way to keep adding to your landscape design. You can always decorate a cut tree (maybe a smaller tabletop version) to extend the period of your holiday decorations. Planted trees should be watered thoroughly and sprayed with an antidesiccant.

Index

Picture Credits

The editors are grateful to all the photographers and archivists who contributed to this book. Special thanks to Tina Anderson, photo editor of *Country Living* magazine.

Cover photo by Steven Randazzo.

"Inside" decorative panel photo by Keith Scott Morton. All other decorative panels from Fair Street Pictures.

Pages v, vi, vii; Photographs courtesy of the author; 2, Jim Bastardo; 5, Robert Bull; 6, Private Collection; 7, Paul Whichloe; 8, Jim Bastardo; 10, Karen Bussolini; 11, Paul Rocheleau Photography; 12, Fair Street Pictures; 13, Keith Scott Morton; 14, Private Collection; 16, Fair Street Pictures; 17, Keith Scott Morton; 18, Karen Bussolini; 19, Fair Street Pictures; 21, Robert Bull; 22, Fair Street Pictures; 23, William P. Steele; 24, Fair Street Pictures; 25, Hans van Lemmen; 26, The Library of Congress; 27, Max Polster Archive; 28, Private Collection; 29, Ad from Emergence of Advertising in America, Rare Book, Manuscript, & Special Collections Library, Duke University; 30, Fair Street Pictures; 31, Design by Janet Moyer, IALD. Photo by Kenneth Rice; 32, Steve Randazzo; 33, Jerry Pavia; 35, Robert Bull; 36, Steven Randazzo; 37, Fair Street Pictures; 38, Picture Collection, The Branch Libraries, The New York Public Library; 39, Condé Nast, *House & Garden*, January 1927; 40, Fair Street Pictures; 41-42, Jessie Walker; 43, Keith Scott Morton; 44, Paul Rocheleau Photography; 45, Fair Street Pictures; 46, Keith Scott Morton; 47, Michael Melford Photography; 48, Helen Norman; 51, Robert Bull; 52 Left, Michael Luppino; 52 Right, Keith Scott Morton; 53, William P. Steele; 54, Fair Street Pictures; 56, Keith Scott Morton; 58, Paul Rocheleau Photography; 59, Condé Nast, *House & Garden,* January 1930; 60, William P. Steele; 61, Fair Street Pictures; 62-63, Courtesy of Craftsman® tools, www.sears.com/craftsman; 64, Fair Street Pictures; 65, Michael Melford Photography; 67, Robert Bull; 68, Private Collection; 69, Keith Scott Morton; 70, Pascal Blancon; 71, LAURA FISHER/Antique Quilts & Americana, New York City; 72, David Prince; 73, Keith Scott Morton; 74, The Library of Congress; 75, Keith Scott Morton; 76, Gross & Daley Photography; 77, Private Collection; 78, Mark Lohman; 79, Keith Scott Morton; 80-81, Fair Street Pictures; 83, Robert Bull; 84, Steven Randazzo; 85, Fair Street Pictures; 86, Jeff McNamara; 87, William P. Steele; 88, Michael Melford Photography; 89-90, Max Polster Archive; 91, John Blais;

92-93, Private Collection; 94, Jessie Walker; 95, Fair Street Pictures; 96, The Library of Congress; 98, Ruedi Hofmann; 101, Robert Bull; 102-103, Keith Scott Morton; 104, Private Collection; 105, Siede Preis/Getty Images; 107, Keith Scott Morton; 108 Left, *Fame Weathervane*, Attributed to E.G. Washburne & Company, New York, c. 1890. Copper and zinc with gold leaf, 39 x 35 3/4 x 23 1/2", Collection of American Folk Art Museum, New York, Promised gift of Ralph Esmerian, P1.2001.372. Photo by Gavin Ashworth, New York; 108 Right, Courtesy of Lightning Rod Parts, www.lightningrodparts.com, and Robbins Lightning Rods; 109, Paul Rocheleau Photography; 110, Jim Bastardo; 111, Fair Street Pictures; 112, Charles Mann; 113, Courtesy of W. Atlee Burpee & Co.; 115, Robert Bull; 116, Keith Scott Morton; 118, Michael Luppino; 119, Michael Melford; 120 Left, Fair Street Pictures; 120 Right, William P. Steele; 121, Charles Gold; 122, The Newberry Library, Chicago, Illinois; 123, Fair Street Pictures; 125, Robert Bull; 126, Kari Haavisto; 127, Keith Scott Morton; 128, Picture Collection, The Branch Libraries, The New York Public Library; 130, Private Collection; 131, William P. Steele; 132, The Newberry Library, Chicago, Illinois; 133, Fair Street Pictures; 134, Gridley & Graves Photography; 135, Hagley Museum and Library; 136, Jim Bastardo; 137, Alan & Linda Detrick; 138, Michael Melford Photography; 141, Robert Bull; 142, Ad from Emergence of Advertising in America, Rare Book, Manuscript, & Special Collections Library, Duke University; 143, Michael Luppino; 144, Ad from Emergence of Advertising in America, Rare Book, Manuscript, & Special Collections Library, Duke University; 145, Michael Melford Photography; 146-147, Ad from Emergence of Advertising in America. Rare Book, Manuscript, & Special Collections Library, Duke University; 148, Keith Scott Morton; 149, Michael Melford Photography; 150, Paul Rocheleau Photography; 151, Fair Street Pictures; 152, Alan & Linda Detrick; 153, Painting by Corinne Lapin-Cohen; 155, Robert Bull; 156, Keith Scott Morton; 157, Fair Street Pictures; 158, Michael Melford Photography; 160, Courtesy of Benjamin Moore & Co.; 162, Fair Street Pictures; 163, Keith Scott Morton; 164, Picture Collection, The Branch Libraries, The New York Public Library; 165, Michael Melford Photography; 167, Robert Bull; 168, Al Tuefen; 171, Linda and Alan Detrick; 172, Steve Randazzo; 174, Keith Scott Morton; 175, Hagley Museum and Library; 176, Linda and Alan Detrick; 177, David Prince.